# A TELEGRAM FROM MARCEL DUCHAMP

David Prowler

©1990 Readymade Press • 2nd Edition ©2026

ISBN 979-8-234-01507-5

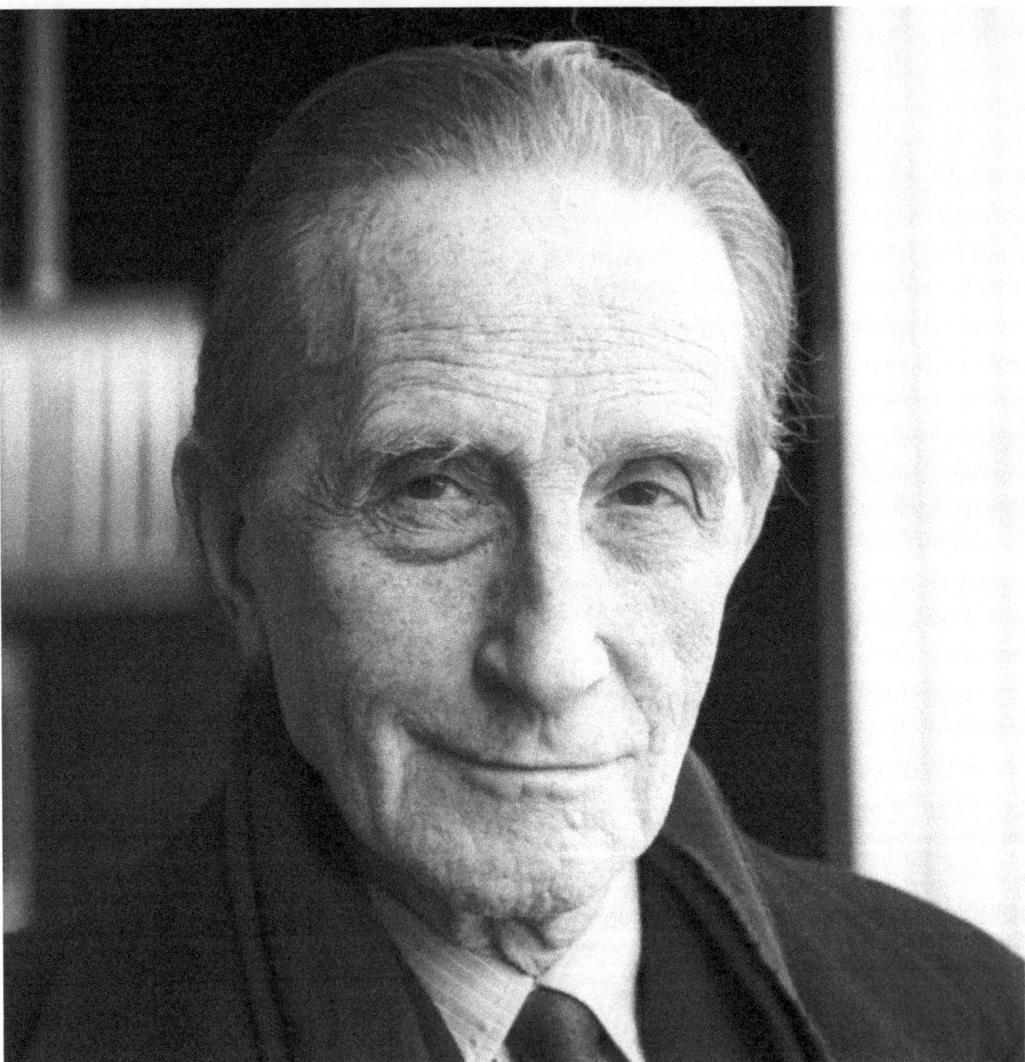

toute mon
amitié
Marcel Duchamp

marcel Duchamp
28 W 10
AL 4 8692

I wanted something signed by Marcel Duchamp.

Something ephemeral, not a collector's item. Just a note or a change of address card or a receipt, something like that, the kind of scrap shed in everyday life.

I called about a dozen autograph dealers and rare book stores in New York, Boston, Philadelphia, San Francisco, New Jersey, and Berkeley. (This was before the Internet.)

In San Francisco I found a signed and numbered book, one of a hundred. A catalogue of a show in 1965 — $950.

Then I found the Telegram.

It's not a signed collector's item produced for the art market. Probably Duchamp never saw or touched it. Yet it is "by" him.

| *Back View* |

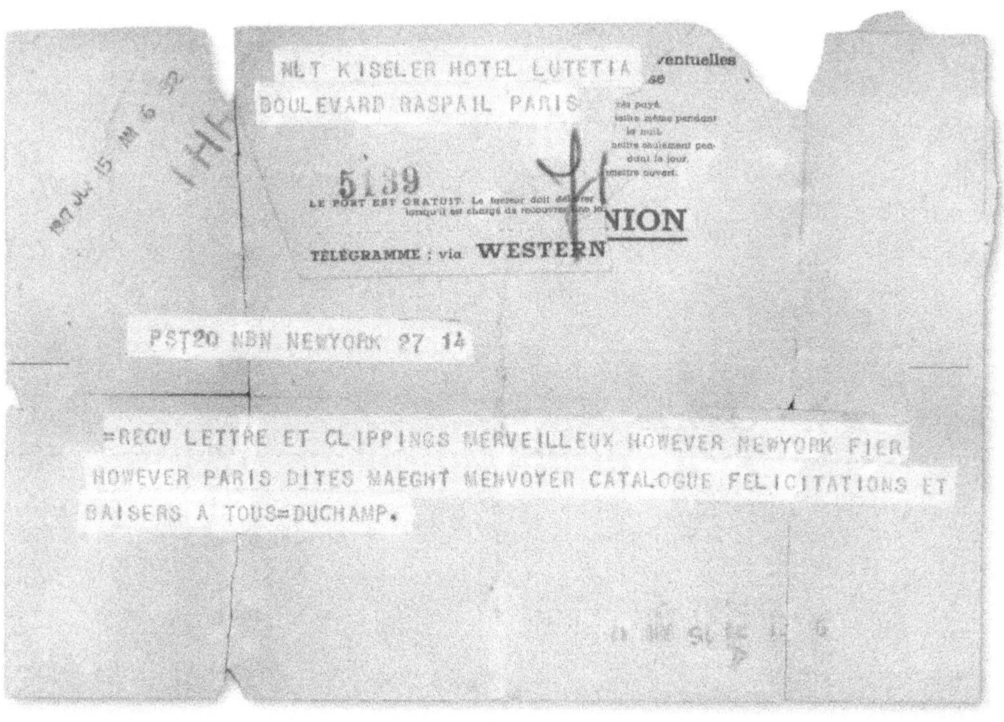


A Telegram From Marcel Duchamp
1947, New York City
•
5 ⁷⁄₈ inches by 8 ⁵⁄₈ inches

| Front View |

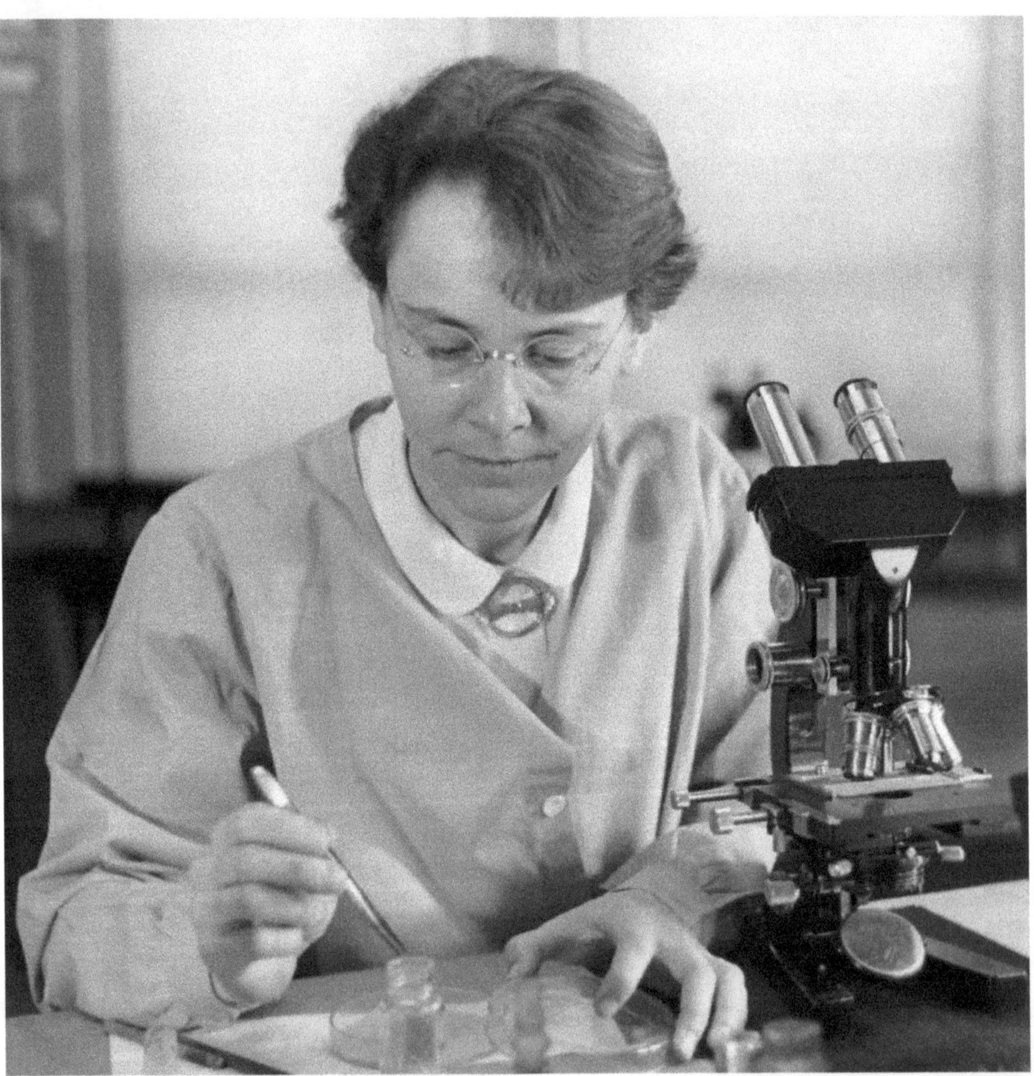

# 5 CHARACTERISTICS OF THE TELEGRAM

1. It is folded in eighths. The upper left eighth is barely attached.

2. It is green, brown, purple, blue, and straw colored.

3. It is a collage.

4. It is at once an original and a mechanical reproduction.

5. It's been folded, carried, handled, sent, delivered, received, and saved.

"RECEIVED LETTER AND MARVELOUS CLIPPINGS
HOWEVER NEW YORK PROUD HOWEVER TELL MAEGHT
TO SEND ME CATALOGUE CONGRATULATIONS AND
KISSES TO ALL = DUCHAMP."

Refers to Frederick J. Kiesler, architect, author, artist.

The Kieslers were in Paris for the exhibition "*Le Surréalisme en 1947.*"

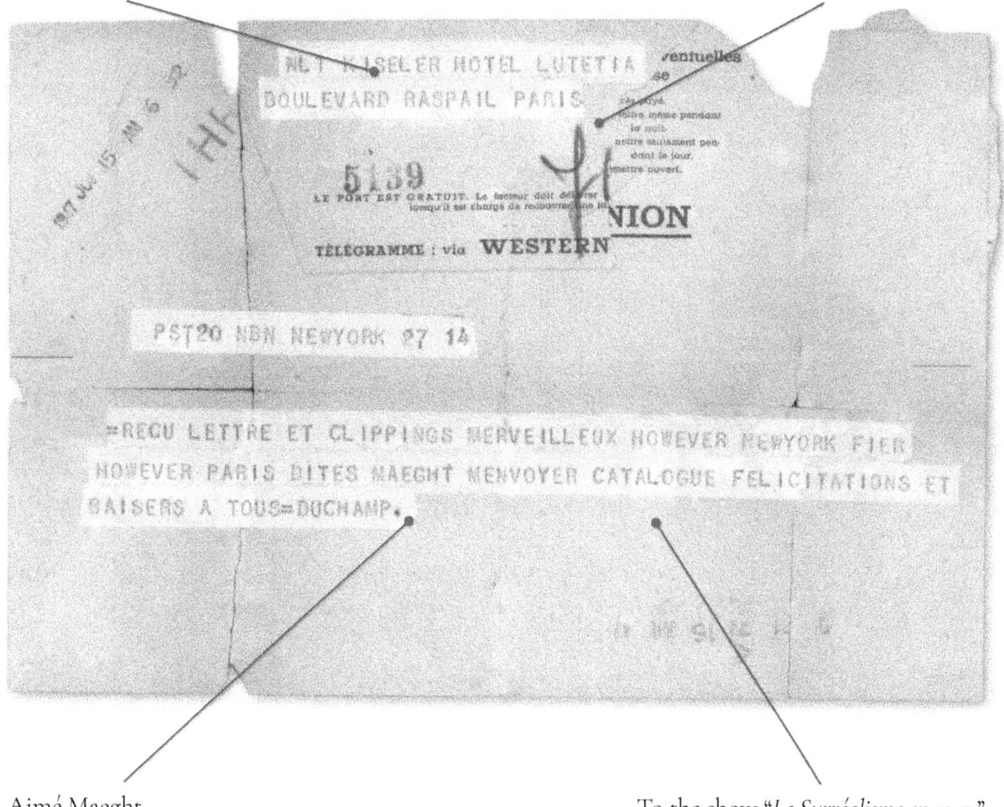


Aimé Maeght, gallery owner and publisher.

To the show "*Le Surréalisme en 1947.*" Designed by Kiesler, show ran at the Gallerie Maeght, 13 Rue de Teheran, from July–August 1947.

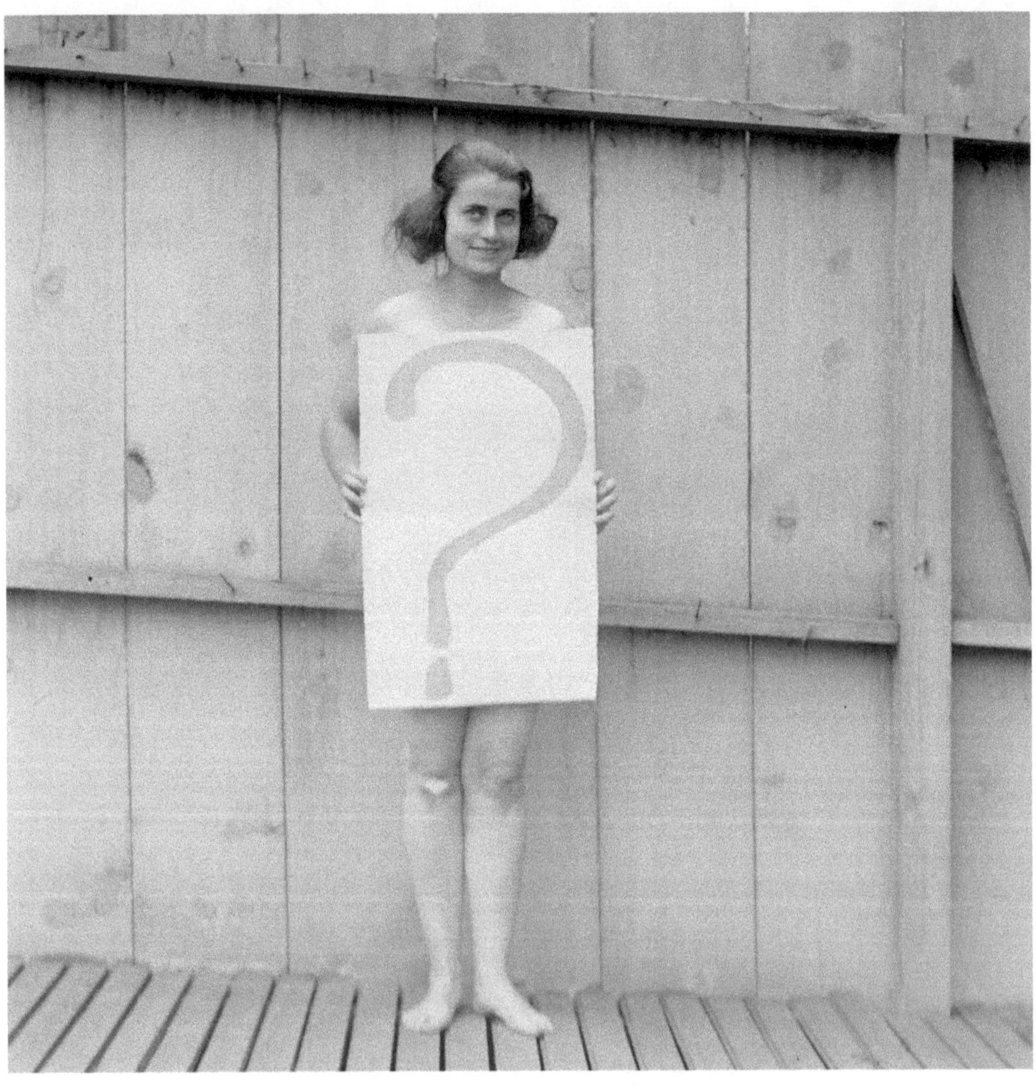

# MEANING

What does the Telegram mean?

It refers to some press clippings Kiesler sent Duchamp from Paris about the show Le Surréalisme en 1947. Duchamp liked the clippings and asked for a copy of the catalogue.

But what is this about: "New York fier (proud) however Paris"?  And why "Kiseler" instead of Kiesler?

Maybe it meant something to Duchamp and Kiesler, but more likely the transmission got mixed up or a clerk misunderstood.

Chance got in the way.

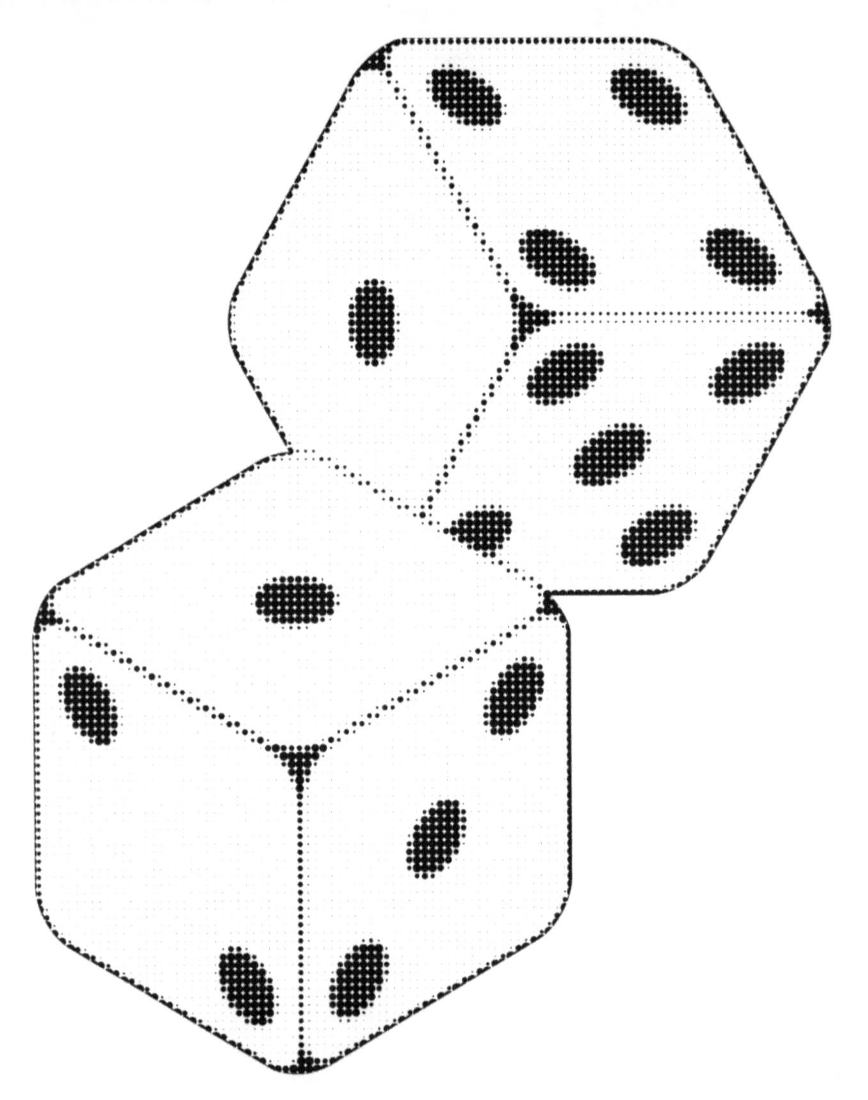

# CHANCE

Duchamp appreciated chance and based many important works on it. *Three Standard Stoppages* was a set of wooden forms whose shapes were determined by falling string: three one-meter strings dropped one meter. In *The Bride Stripped Bare by her Bachelors, Even* (*La Mariée Mise à Nu Par ses Célibataires, Même)* he used the unpredictable patterns of dust formation. And when the 9-foot-tall glass sculpture broke, he was delighted and protected the cracks.

A gambler, he devised a method to beat chance at Monte Carlo. The goal was to break even. He spoke of "canned chance" and "the regime of coincidence".

•

"Your chance is not the same as mine, just as your throw of the dice will rarely be the same as mine."

*–Marcel Duchamp*

# Les Girafes

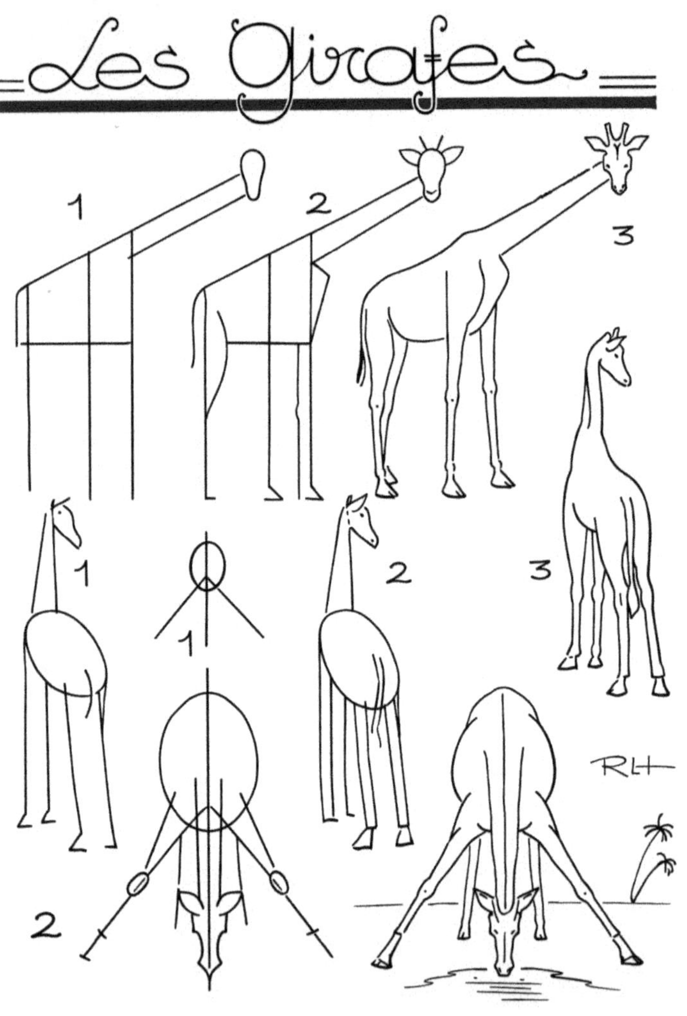

# DIGNITY

"Readymades are manufactured objects promoted to the dignity of objects of art through the choice of the artist."

*–André Breton*

In this regard, the artist is like Midas, touching things and turning them to gold, or a shaman imbuing twigs with power.

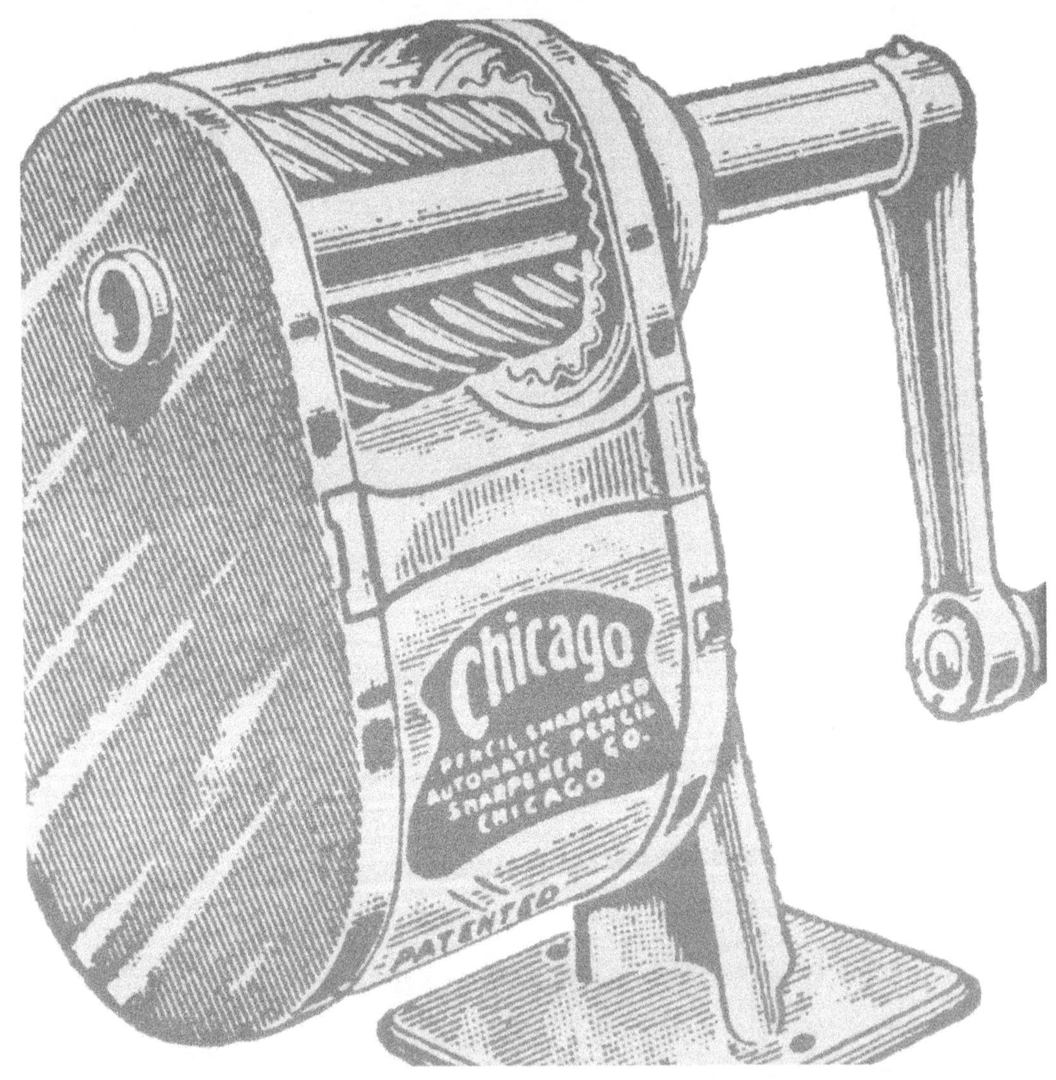

Chicago
PENCIL SHARPENED
AUTOMATIC PENCIL
SHARPENER CO.
CHICAGO
PATENTED

# INTEREST

"It is very difficult to select an object that has absolutely no interest for us not only on the day we pick it but that never will and that, finally, can never have the possibility of becoming beautiful, pretty, agreeable, or ugly."

*—Marcel Duchamp*

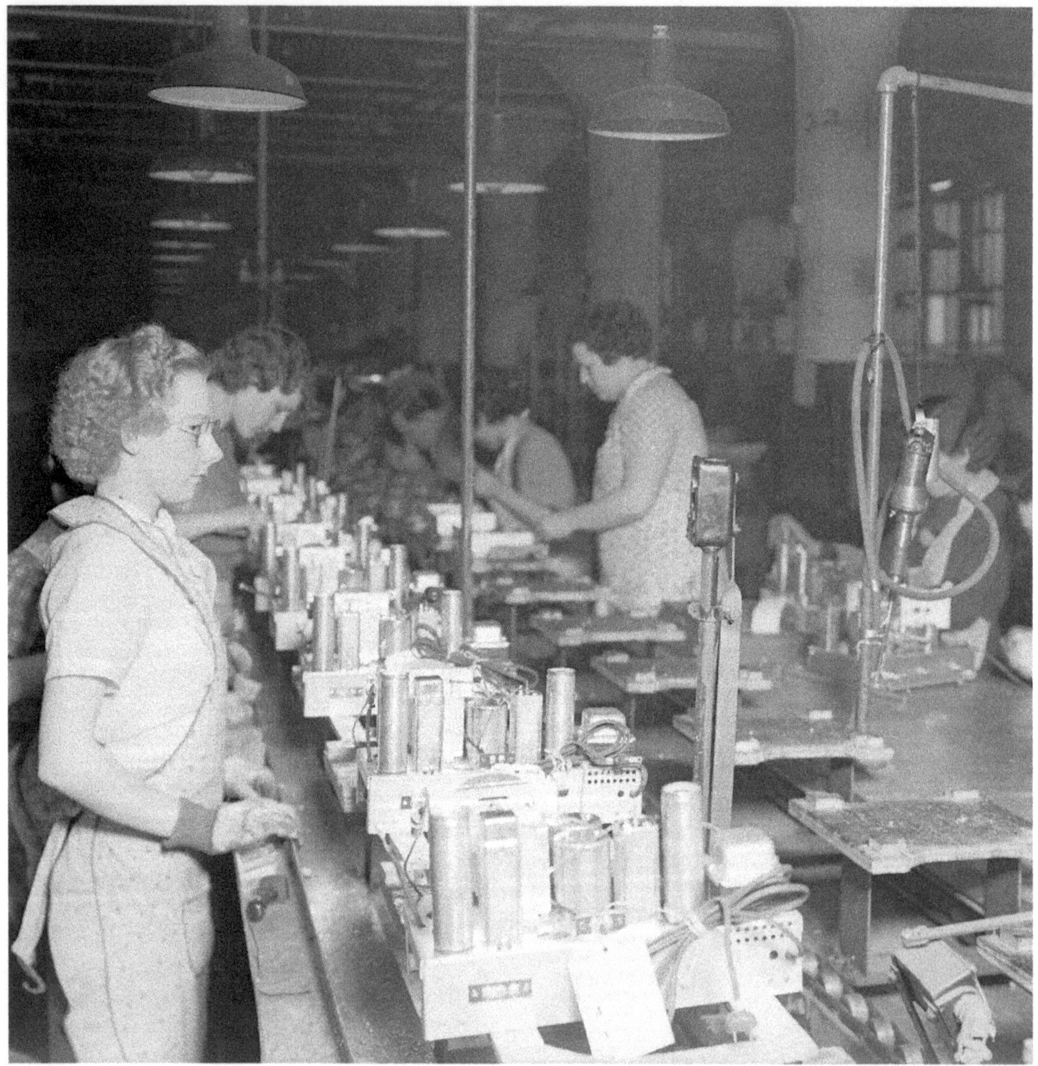

"Peut-on faire des choses qui ne sont pas de l'art?"
(Can one make things that are not art?)

–*Marcel Duchamp*


"I want something where the eye and hand count
for nothing."

–*Marcel Duchamp*

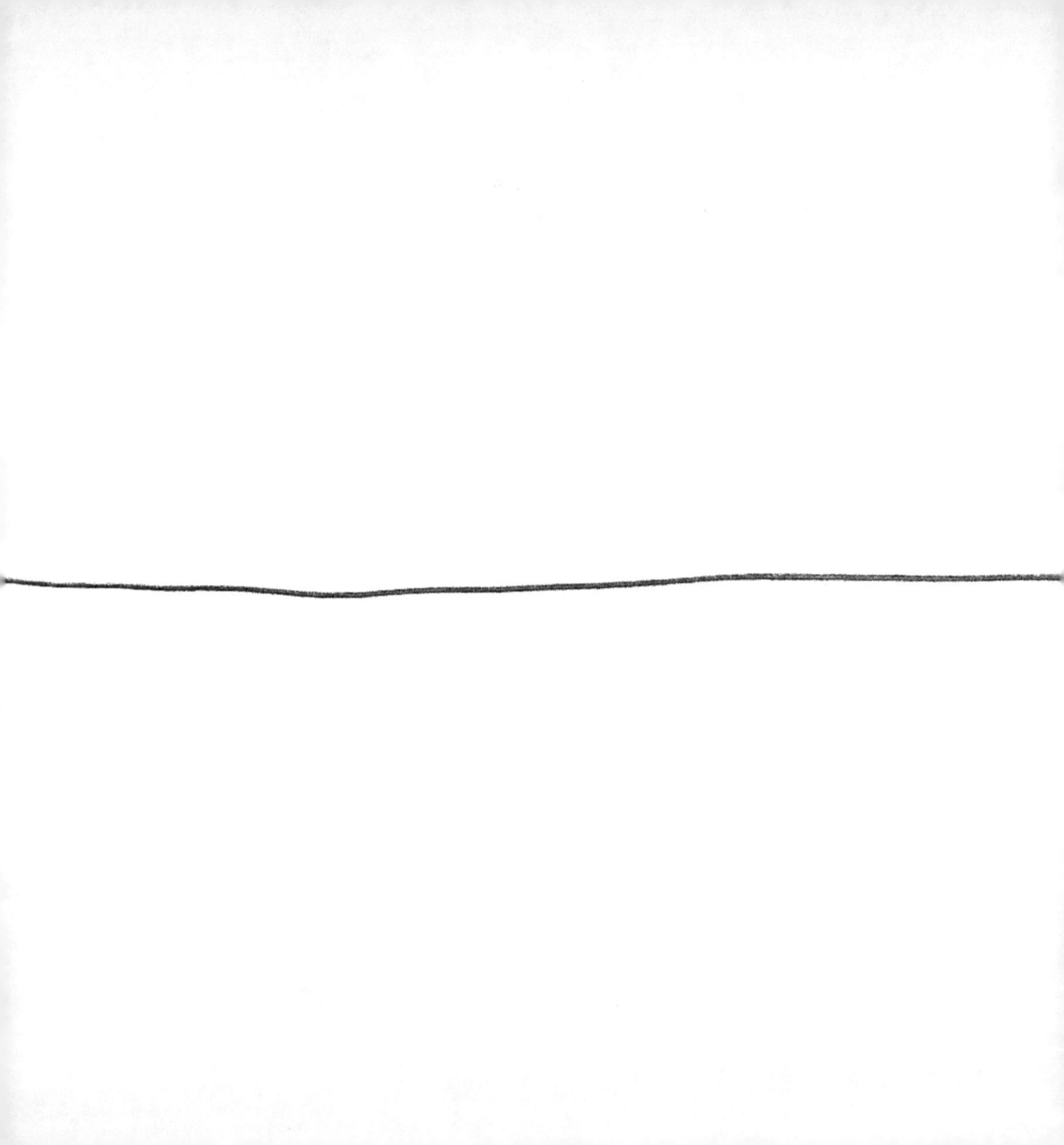

## INDIFFERENCE

"The choice of these Readymades was never dictated by an aesthetic delectation. The choice was based on a reaction of visual indifference with at the same time a total absence of good or bad taste, in fact a complete anesthesia."

*–Marcel Duchamp*

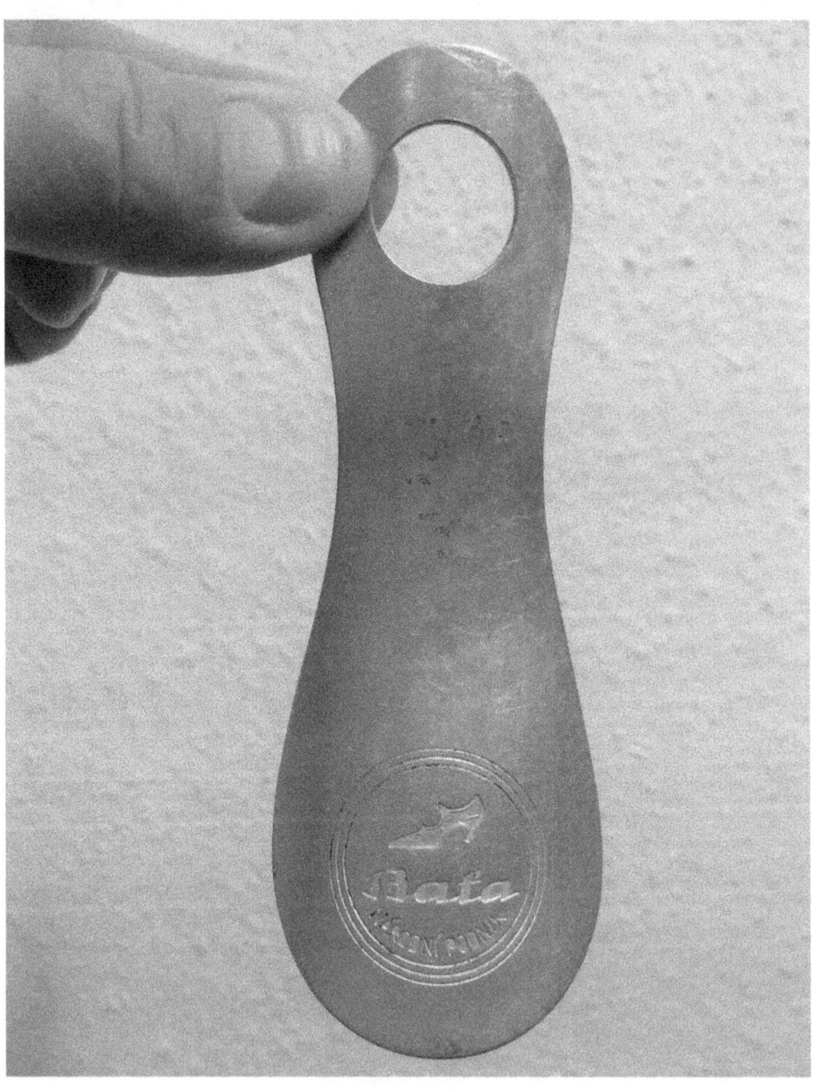
Bata

## CHOICE

The artist chooses a bowl of apples or a field of wheat with crows circling overhead or a nude woman sitting on the edge of a bed looking at a square of light on the floor or a rich man with his possessions or Jesus Christ or a can of soup.

The artist picks a thing and says, "Look at this."

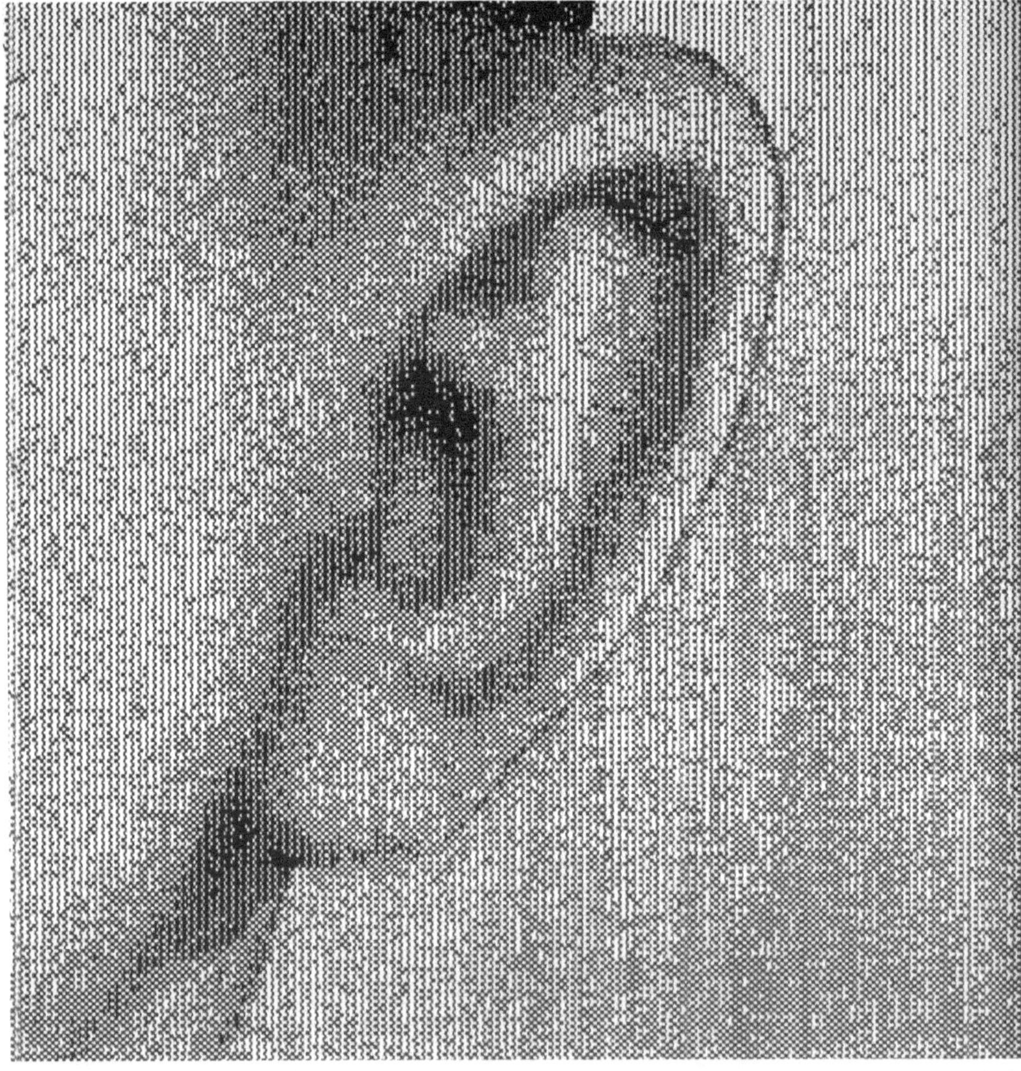

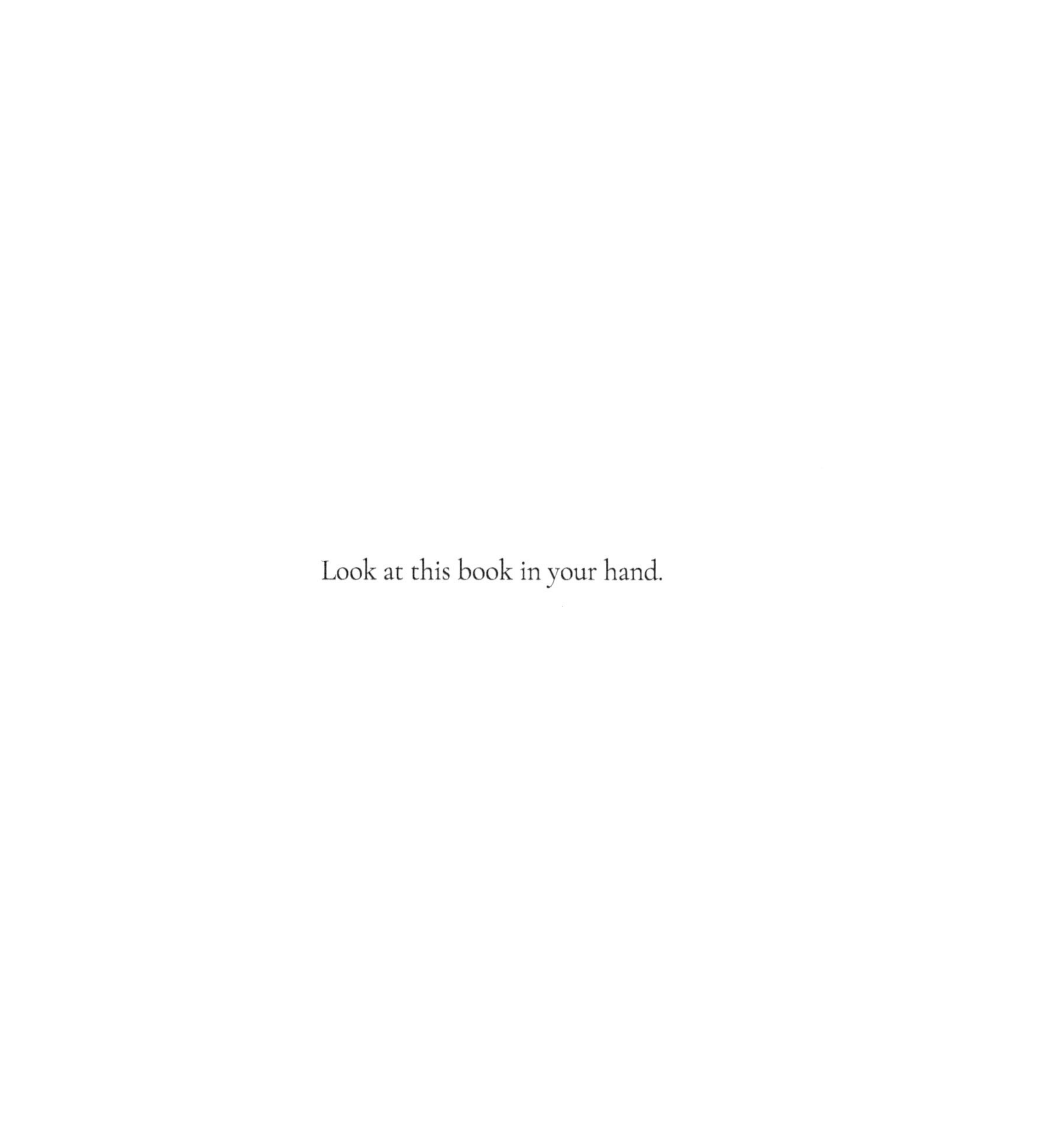

Look at this book in your hand.

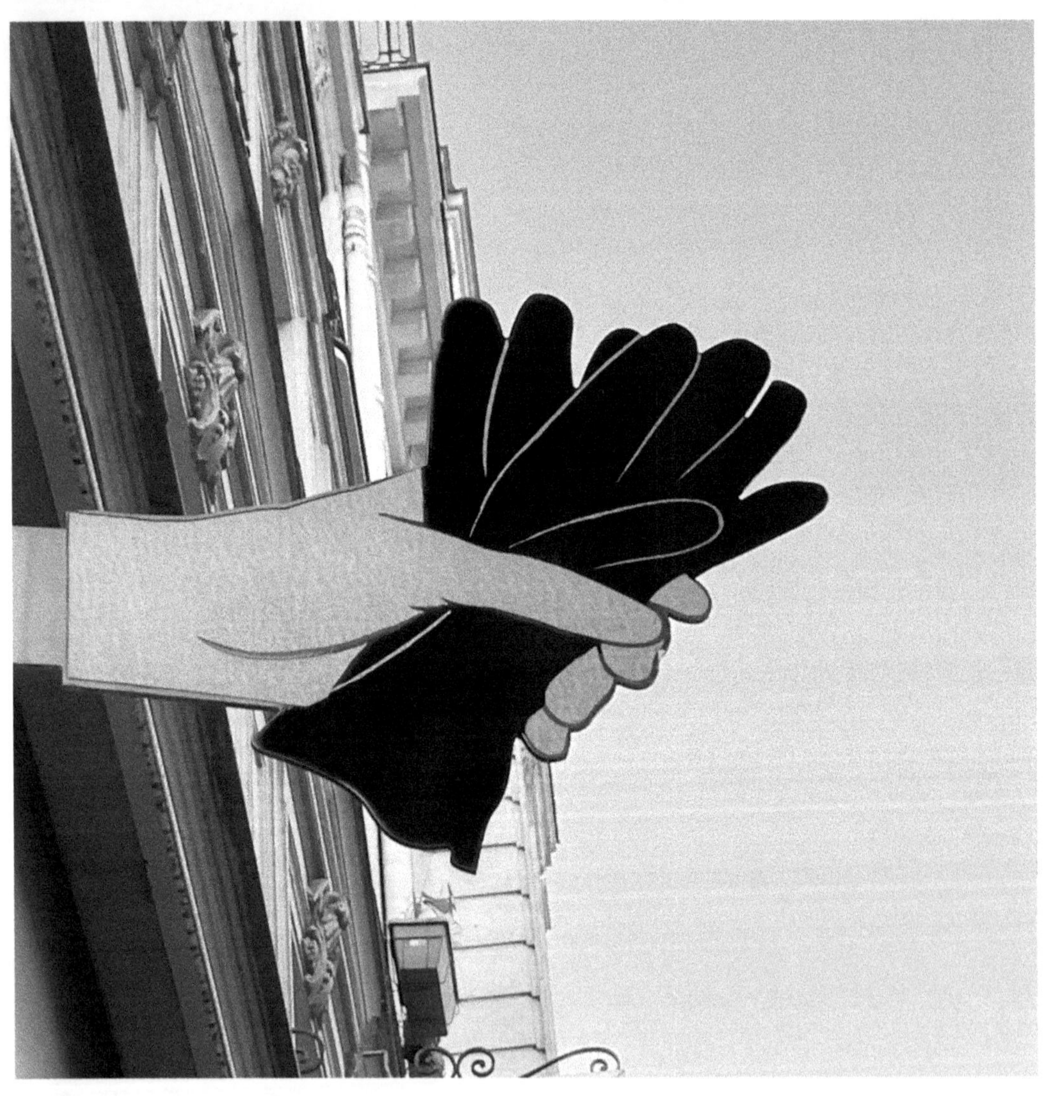

## DUCHAMP CHOSE:

- ☑ A bicycle wheel in 1913

- ☑ A bottle rack in 1914

- ☑ A shovel in 1915

- ☑ A comb in 1916

- ☑ A typewriter cover in 1916

- ☑ A urinal in 1917

"Whether Mr. Mutt with his own hands made them or
not has no importance. He chose them."

*–Marcel Duchamp*

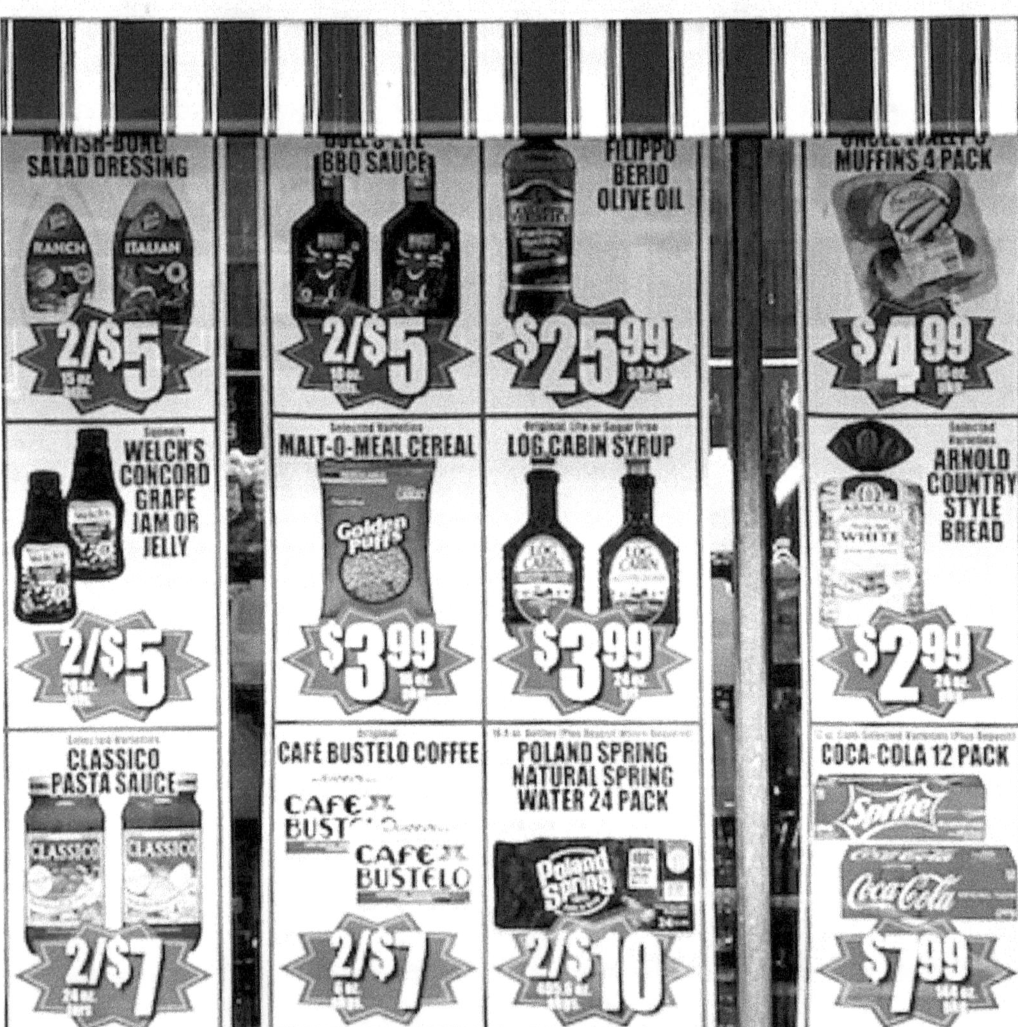
WISH-BONE SALAD DRESSING
RANCH
ITALIAN
2/$5
BULL'S EYE BBQ SAUCE
2/$5
FILIPPO BERIO OLIVE OIL
$25.99
UNCLE WALLY'S MUFFINS 4 PACK
$4.99
WELCH'S CONCORD GRAPE JAM OR JELLY
2/$5
MALT-O-MEAL CEREAL
Golden Puffs
$3.99
LOG CABIN SYRUP
$3.99
ARNOLD COUNTRY STYLE BREAD
WHITE
$2.99
CLASSICO PASTA SAUCE
CLASSICO
CLASSICO
2/$7
CAFÉ BUSTELO COFFEE
CAFÉ BUSTELO
CAFÉ BUSTELO
2/$7
POLAND SPRING NATURAL SPRING WATER 24 PACK
Poland Spring
2/$10
COCA-COLA 12 PACK
Sprite
Coca-Cola
$7.99

# YOU CHOOSE

This is:

- [ ] a book about a telegram
- [ ] a book about an artist
- [ ] a book about an artwork
- [ ] a work of art
- [ ] a product
- [ ] all of the above
- [ ] none of the above

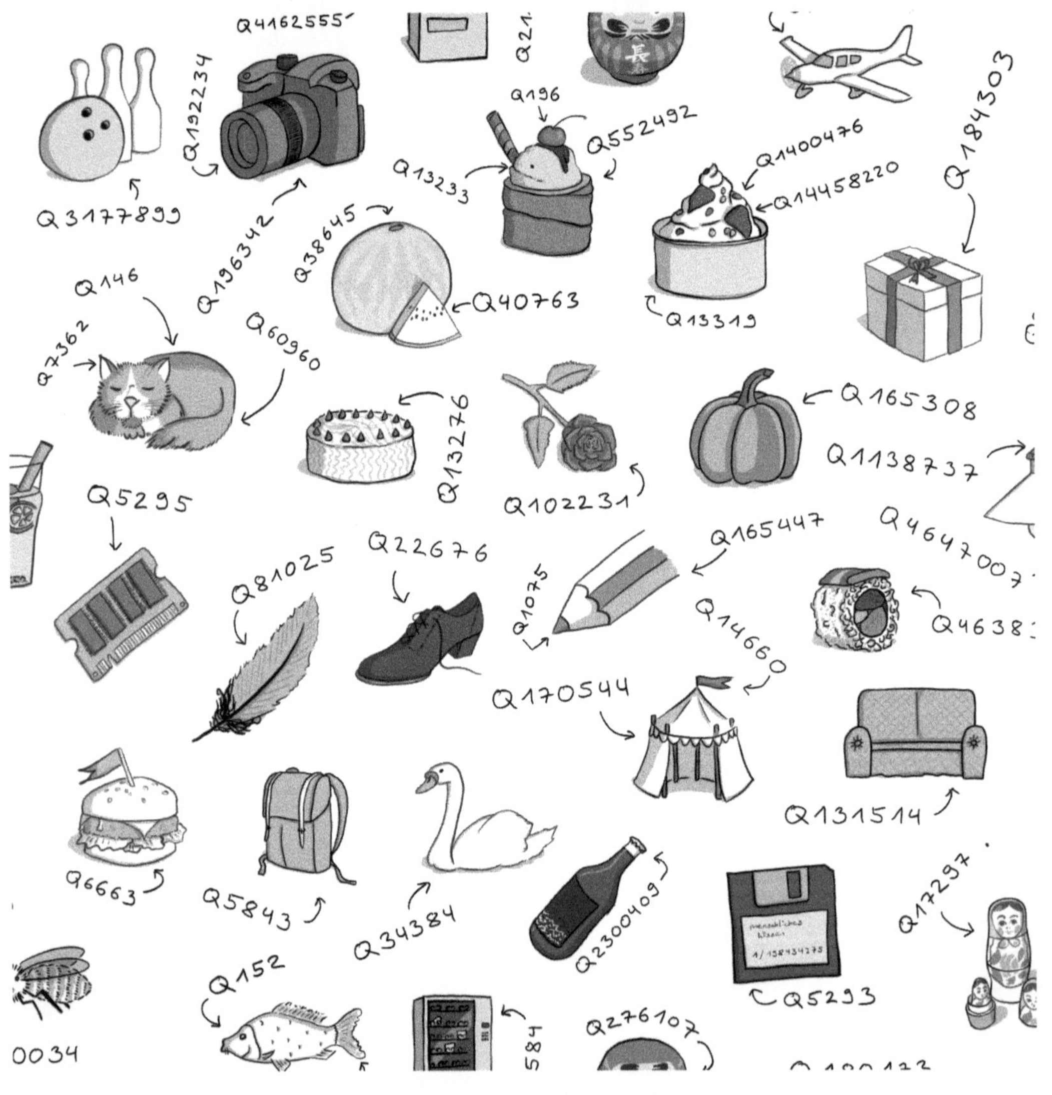

Q4162555
Q192234
Q3177899
Q196342
Q146
Q7362
Q146
Q196
Q552492
Q13233
Q38645
Q60960
Q40763
Q1400476
Q14458220
Q13319
Q184303
Q5295
Q13276
Q102231
Q165308
Q1138737
Q81025
Q22676
Q1075
Q165447
Q4647007
Q4638
Q170544
Q14660
Q6663
Q5843
Q152
Q34384
Q2300409
Q276107
Q5293
Q17297
Q131514
0034
584

This page is for you to draw or paste a picture of the object of your choice.

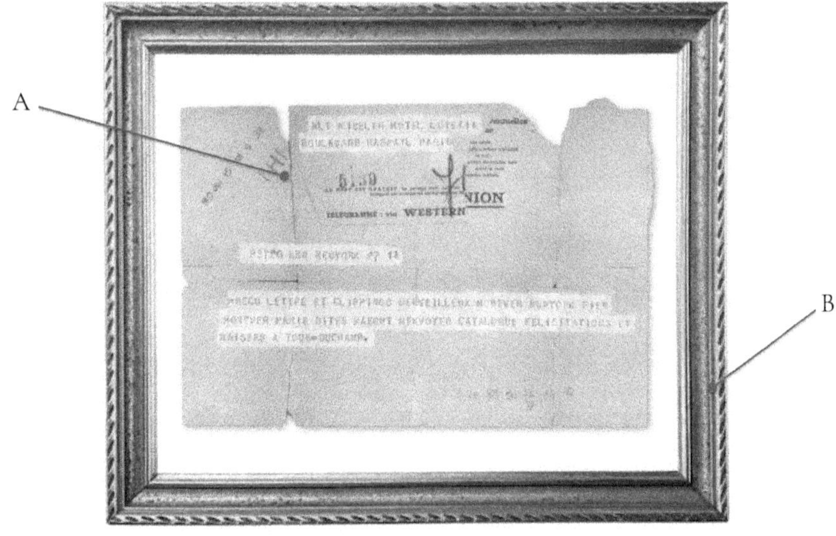

A
B

# ART

Is it

☐ A

☐ B

☐ A+B

☐ None of the above

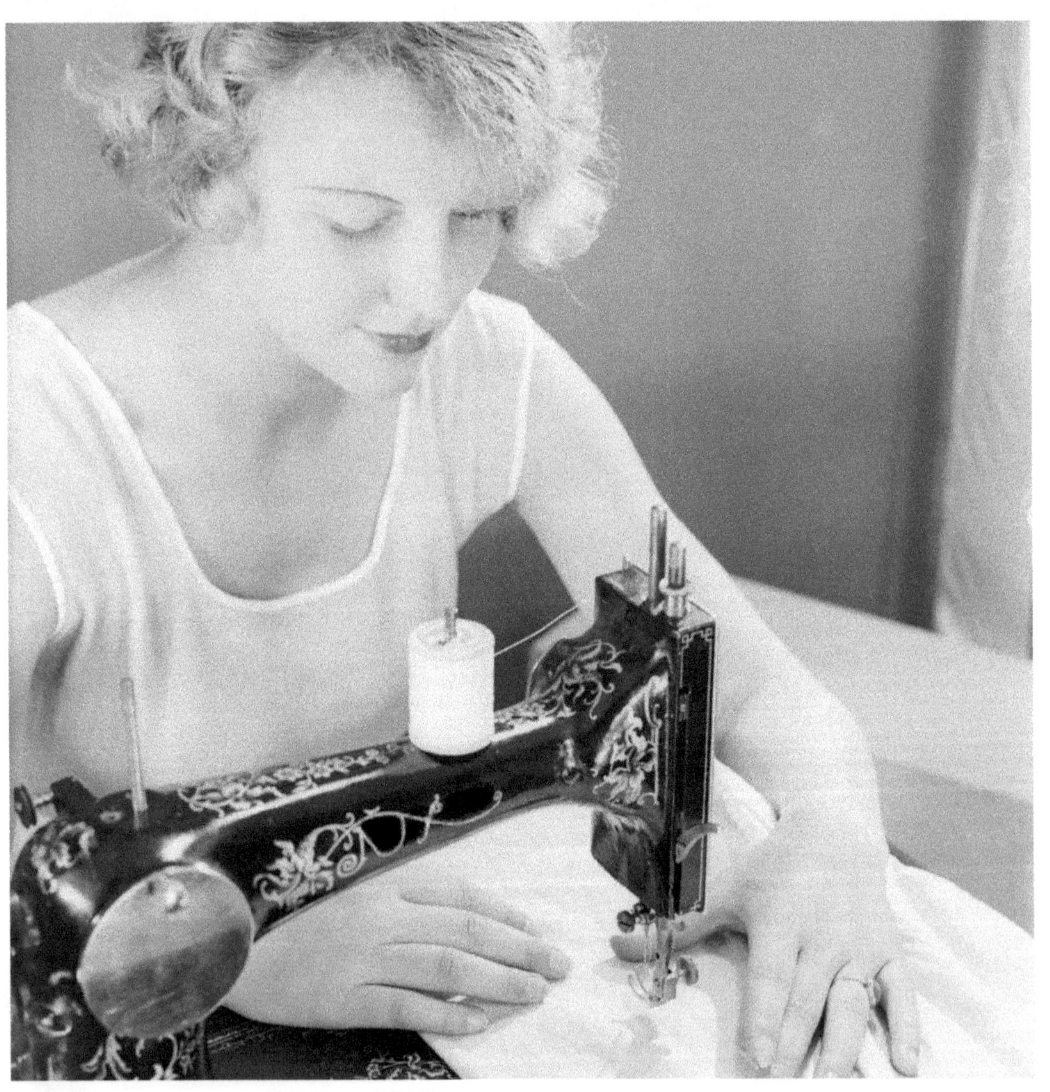

# NOT A READYMADE

The Readymades have artistic intent.

They were not made by Duchamp.

The Telegram is by Duchamp but without artistic intent.

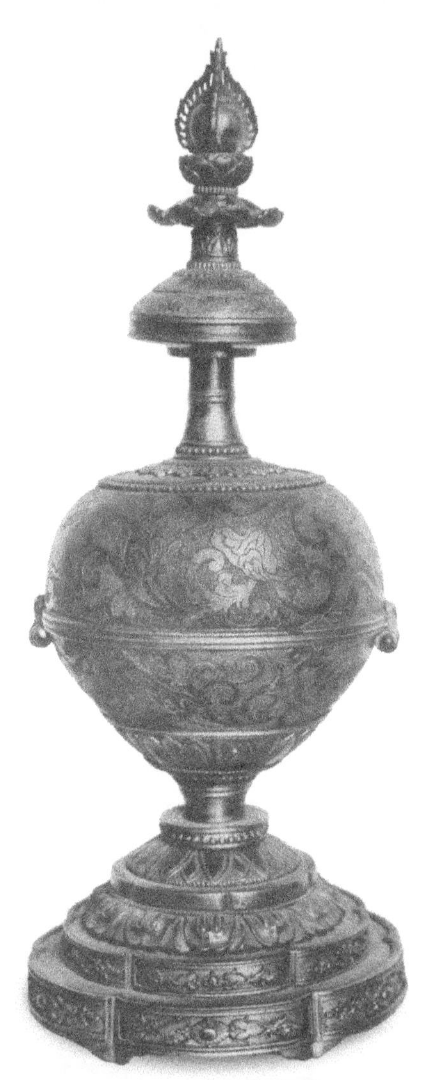

# POSSESSION

Why would anyone want to own the Telegram?

Would it be like possessing a relic of a saint or a lock of Elvis's hair?

Maybe it would create a bond between the owner and the dead artist.

Can such a bond be bought and sold?

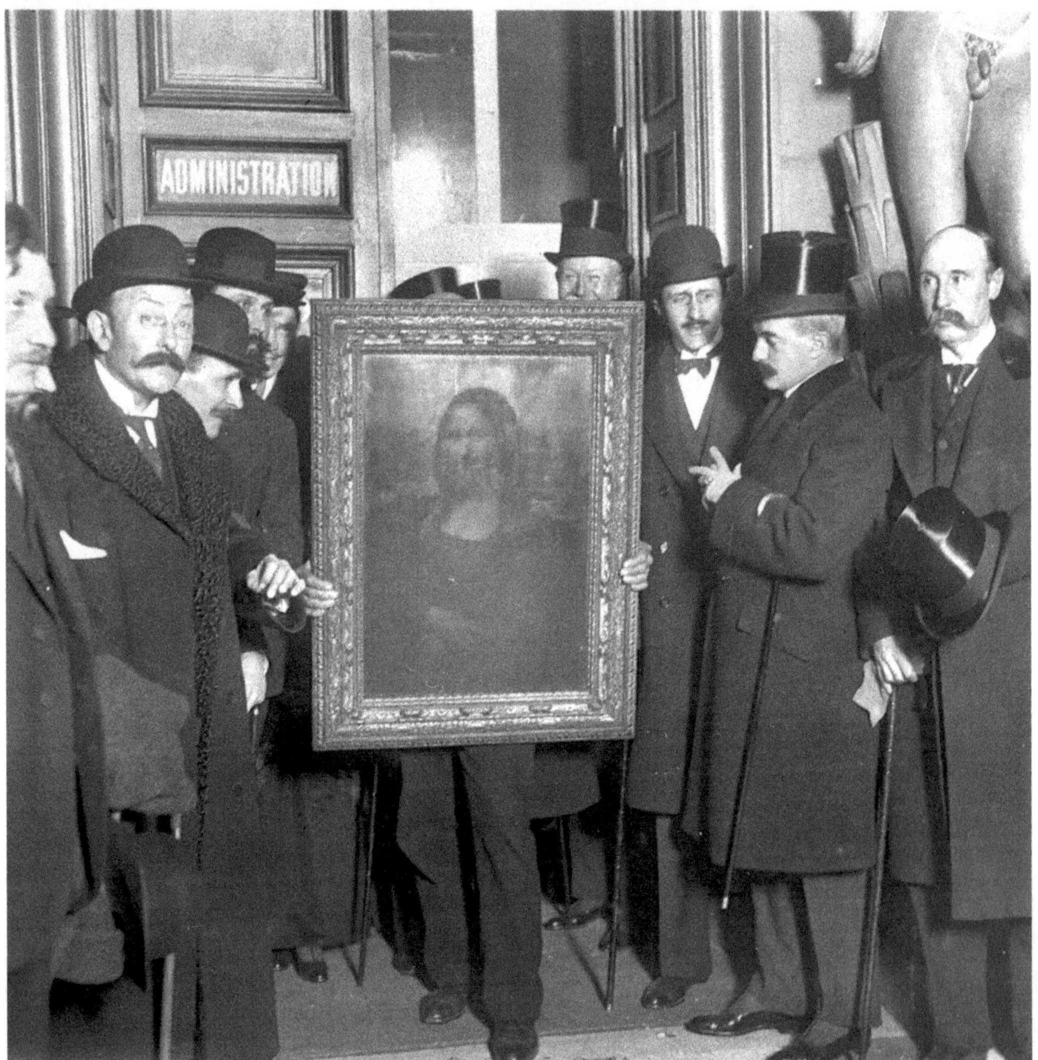
ADMINISTRATION

# VALUE

The Telegram is a commodity, available for purchase. The seller is asking $350. Is this the Telegram's value?

Now this book has been published about the Telegram. Is it worth more?

What if Duchamp had signed it? As you know, he took everyday objects and when he added his signature their values skyrocketed. They became Art.

And what would be the value of that signature without the Telegram, just by itself?

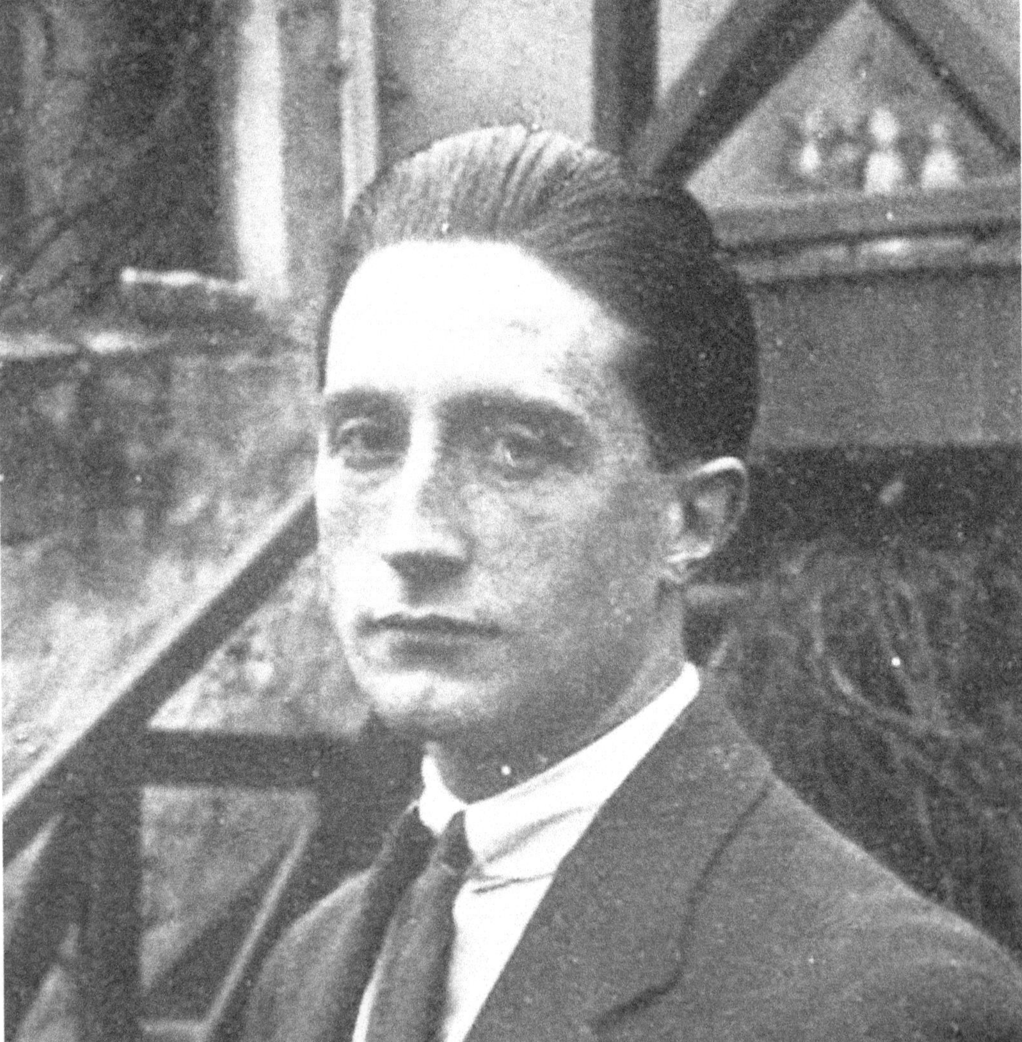

## BELIEF

We believe that Marcel Duchamp, the famous artist, wrote the Telegram and on July 15, 1947 sent it from New York City to Paris. We believe that the piece of paper that is the subject of this book is that telegram written by Duchamp and sent from New York City to Paris on July 15, 1947.

Why do we believe this?

"Q: What do you believe in?

Duchamp: Nothing of course! The word belief is another error. It's like the word judgment. They're both horrible ideas, on which the world is based. I hope it won't be like this on the moon.

Q: Nevertheless, you believe in yourself?

Duchamp: No."

```
X

                    POUR VOS DEPOTS DE TELEGRAMMES

            LE C.I.P.B  A VOTRE SERVICE TOUS LES JOURS 24H/24H


- PAR TELEPHONE DEPUIS L'ILE DE FRANCE AU (1) 4233.4411


- PAR TELEX AU 250500 OU PAR MINITEL AU (1) 4233.1666
  (REDUCTION D'ENVIRON 20-0/0) - RENSEIGNEMENTS AU 0519.3333



ZCZC XP0123 UDF362 IOA104 1-0058451064
FRXX CO UDNX 042 TF 45434593 TELEPHONE PAR PARIS-CIPB LE  6 A 0717
TDWX BRIDGETON MO 42/41 05 1525


C NICOLAS
137 RUE DALESIA
75014PARISFRANCE


NLT KISELER HOTEL LUTETIA
BOULEVARD RAISPAIL PARIS
PST 20 NBN NEWYORK 27 14 RECU LETTRE ET CLIPPINGS MARVELLEUX
HOWEVER NEWYORK FIER HOWEVER PARIS
DITES MAEGHT MENVOYER CATALOGUE FELICITATIONS ET BAISERS A TOUS
   DUCHAMP
TINC


COL   137 75014 20 27 14
```

# REPRODUCTION

In 1964, Duchamp authorized reproductions of the bicycle wheel, bottle rack, shovel, comb, typewriter cover, and urinal.

In 1990, I authorized a reproduction of the Telegram, to be sent like the original 43 years earlier, by Western Union from New York to Paris.

When I had found the original Telegram, I thought: This is it, the object without aesthetic interest.

But when I saw what telegrams looked like in 1990 I realized that the original was in fact beautiful.

# COLLABORATION 1

Robert Prowler, NYC
March 7, 1990, letter

Dear David:

First: Enclosed is a receipt for sending Western Union telegram to Nicolas. The WU office looked like an Off-track Betting office at its worst. Probably people sending or receiving much-needed cash. Bad news, I guess, comes by telephone these days. I had a long consultation with the Western Union man and he assures me it will get there – never mind that the address might be wrong. He proofread all the copy as did I. I hope it is as you wanted and perhaps you have received a fax from Nicolas by now. Keep me posted.

Love,

Dad

# COLLABORATION 2

C. Nicolas, Paris
March 8, 1990, fax

Here it is, David!

I hope your dad didn't make any mistake?! It looks pretty weird to me. If it does not fit the bill, don't hesitate, of course. David, even if it is a very minor contribution, we are glad to be associated (a little bit) in this "telegram from Marcel Duchamp" project. Keep us posted!

Much love,

Nicolas

PS: Mailing the telegram back to you today.
Enclosed, a copy of it.

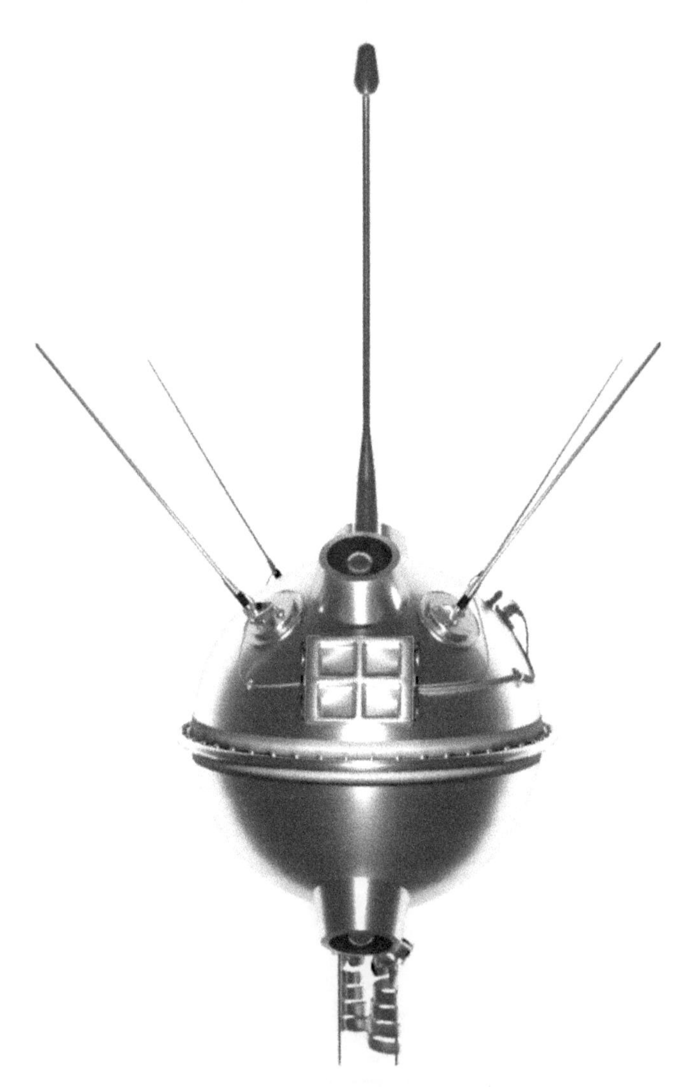

# TRANSMISSION

In 1947 the message went from land to land underwater through a cable.

In 1990 the message was sent from land to land through outer space.

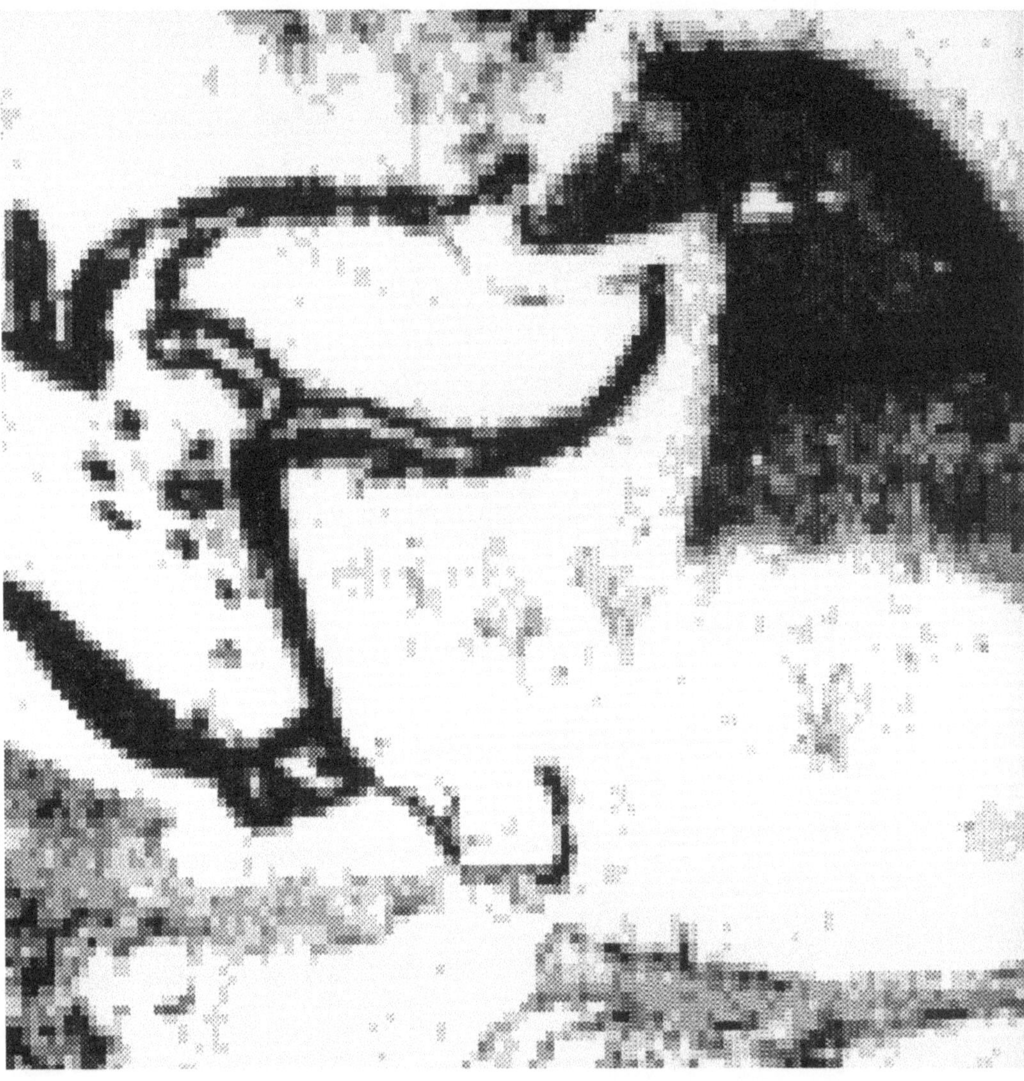

## QUICK ART

"Quick art, that's been the characteristic of the whole century from the Cubists on. The speed that is being used in space, in communications, is also being used in art."

–Marcel Duchamp

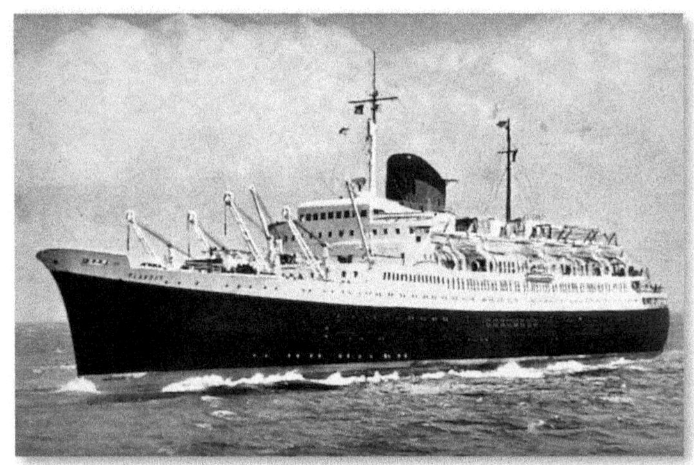

This is not a postcard from Marcel Duchamp.

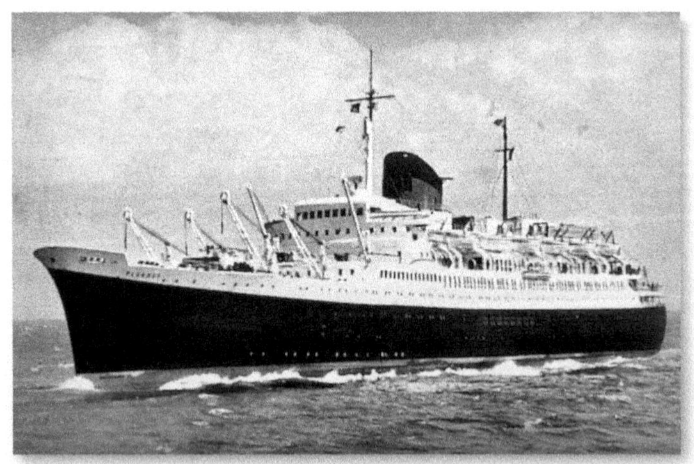

This is a postcard from Marcel Duchamp.

# INFRAMINCE

Duchamp came up with the concept of "inframince", ultra thin.  He gave these examples :

- "The warmth of a seat just left."

- "The odor of smoke that also carries the mouth odor of the smoker."

- "The sound of corduroy trousers rubbing together."

- "The difference between two objects cast from the same mold."

- "The delay between a shot being fired and the bullet hitting its target."

"Figure out the difference between the volumes of air displaced by a clean shirt (ironed and folded) and the same dirty shirt."

–Marcel Duchamp

And what is the difference between a telegram from Marcel Duchamp and another?

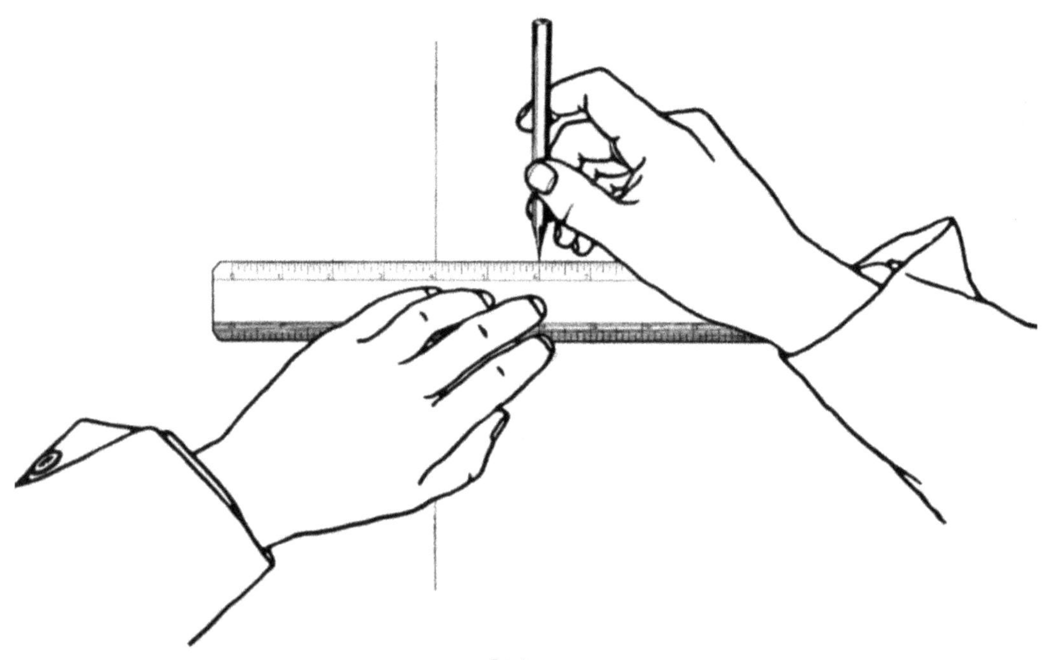

Fig. 8

# EXERCISE

Make sentences about the Telegram using each of these words:

1. Authenticity

2. History

3. Fetish

4. Aesthetics

5. Commodity

6. Idolatry

7. Condition

8. Scarcity

9. Value

# APPENDICES

Art Affidavit

Chronology

Glossary

Frederick J. Kiesler

*Le Surréalisme en 1947*

Superstitions

Gratitude

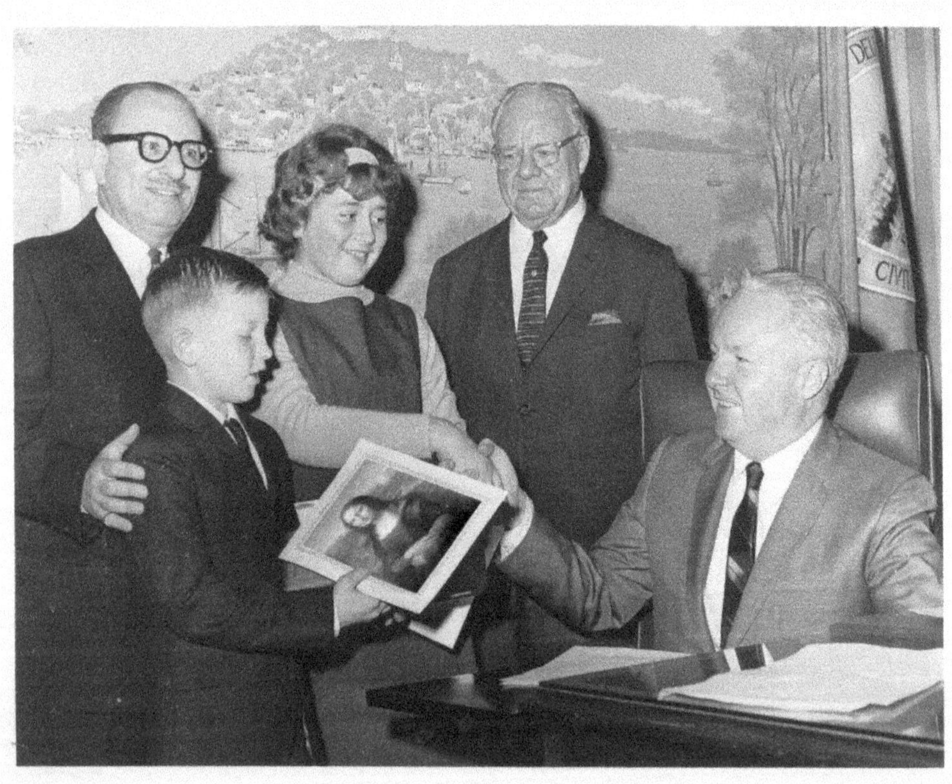

Attestation of Authenticity

I, ___DAVID PROWLER___, being of sound mind and body, hereby declare under penalty of perjury under the laws of the State of California that, to the best of my knowledge and belief, the following exhibits are, by virtue of intrinsic conceptual and aesthetic quality (both advertent and inadvertent), Art.  I have personal knowledge of those matters stated herein and could and would competently testify thereto.

Exhibit A, attached hereto and incorporated herein by this reference thereto, being that certain Western Union telegram (hereinafter referred to as "Telegram" and commonly known as the Duchamp Telegram) sent from the City of New York, State of New York, United States of America to the City of Paris, Country of France, on the date of July 15, 1947.

Exhibit B, attached hereto and incorporated herein by this reference thereto, being that certain telegram sent by Western Union on the date of March 5, 1990 by Robert Prowler from the City of New York, State of New York, United States of America, to C. Nicolas in the City of Paris, Country of France which Exhibit B contained the contents of the aforementioned Telegram.

Exhibit C, incorporated herein by this reference thereto being that certain heretofore unidentified object of art as defined in that certain Webster's New Unabridged Dictionary, copyright 1930 and known personally to the undersigned.

I declare under penalty of perjury under the laws of the State of California that the foregoing is true and correct.
Executed this __29__ day of __March__, 1990 at San Francisco, California.

ACKNOWLEDGEMENT

State of California
County of ___S.F.___

On __3-29-90__, before me, the undersigned, a notary public in and for said state, personally appeared __David Prowler__, personally known to me (or proved to me on the basis of satisfactory evidence) to be the person who executed the within instrument.

Notary Public



STATEMENT BY COUNSEL OF RECORD

This Attestation of Authenticity conforms with the requirements of local ordinances, complies with state law and is not in conflict with applicable federal regulations.

Attorney of Record

1

# CHRONOLOGY

**1887**  Birth of Henri-Robert-Marcel Duchamp in Seine-Maritime, Normandy, France

**1905**  Exempted from military service as an art worker

**1912**  Paints *Nude Descending a Staircase*

**1913**  Abandons painting and begins work on the Large Glass

**1918**  Moves to Argentina for 9 months

**1919**  Has hair cut in the shape of a comet

**1919**  Furnishes Mona Lisa with mustache and goatee

**1920**  Adopts drag persona Rrose Selavy (Eros, c'est la vie)

**1923**  Abandons work on the Large Glass

**1924**  Invents system to break even at Monte Carlo

**1932**  Coins the term "mobile" for Alexander Calder's moving sculptures

**1935**   Captains the French team of the 1st
International Chess by Correspondence Olympiad

**1936**   Visits Cleveland. Returns to France.

**1944**   Begins work on *Étant Donnés*, a diorama to be seen
through two eyeholes in a wooden door. He will
work on this piece in secret for 20 years.

**1947**   SENDS TELEGRAM

**1954**   Marries Alexina "Teeny" Sattler Matisse

**1959**   Becomes a member of the Collège de
Pataphysique in Paris. His rank is the highest
given: Transcendent Satrap, Maître de l'Ordre de
la Grande Gidouille

**1968**   After a dinner party on October 2 with Man Ray
and others, dies peacefully.

At his request, his tombstone reads:

"D'ailleurs c'est toujours les autres qui meurent"
*Besides, it is always the others who die.*

# GLOSSARY

Definitions from Webster's New International Dictionary of the English Language, 1930 edition.

**Art**: Skill, dexterity, or the power of performing certain actions acquired by experience, study, or observation, knack

**Belief**: A state or habit of mind in which trust, confidence, or reliance is placed in some person or thing; confidence; faith

**Chance**: The happening of events; the way in which things befall; fortune. Something that befalls as the result of unknown or unconsidered forces

**Choice**: Act of choosing; the voluntary act of selecting or separating from two or more things that which is preferred

**Chronology**: The science which treats of measuring time by regular divisions or periods, and which assigns to events or transactions their proper dates

**Collaboration**: Act of collaborating or working together; united labor

**Dignity**: State, characteristic, or quality of being worthy or honorable; elevation of character; worth; nobleness; excellence

**Indifference**: Lack of feeling for or against anything; absence of anxiety or interest in respect to anything; unconcernedness

**Glossary**: A collection of glosses; or explanations of words and passages of a work or author; a partial dictionary of a work

**Gratitude**: State of being grateful; warm and friendly feelings toward a benefactor; kindness awakened by a favor received

**Meaning**: That which is meant or intended; intent; purpose

**Possession**: Act or state of having; also thing possessed

**Readymade**: Made already or beforehand, in anticipation of need; lacking originality or individuality

**Reproduction**: Act or process of reproducing; as the reproduction of prosperity; the reproduction by an animal of a lost part

**Transmission**: Act of transmitting; or state of being transmitted; as, the transmission of letters, news, and the like

**Value**: Power which an object confers upon its possessor to command the commodities and services of others. A price which can actually be obtained. The value of an object depends not upon its total utility but its marginal utility, diminishing as the supply increases. Esteem, regard

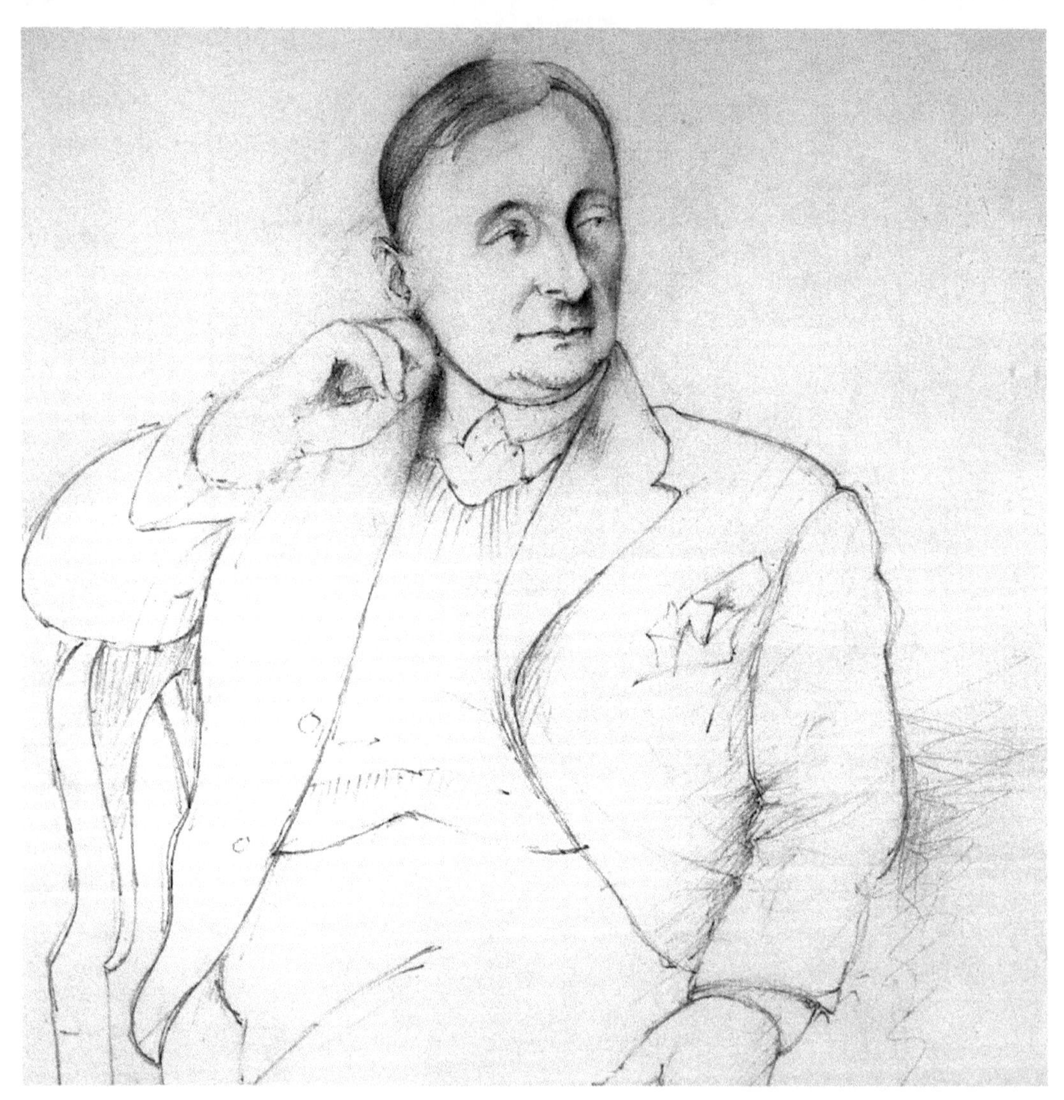

Portrait by Arshile Gorky

## FREDERICK J. KIESLER

The Telegram was sent to Frederick Kiesler. Duchamp believed that the viewer completes the artwork, so Kiesler completed the Telegram just as you are completing this book.

Kiesler was an architect and he designed shop windows, theaters and theatre sets, furniture, and art exhibits. He wrote books on product displays, journals, and poetry. He sculpted and he made films. In 1947, Architectural Forum called him "Design's Bad Boy"

He was CBS's "Architect of the Year" in 1951.

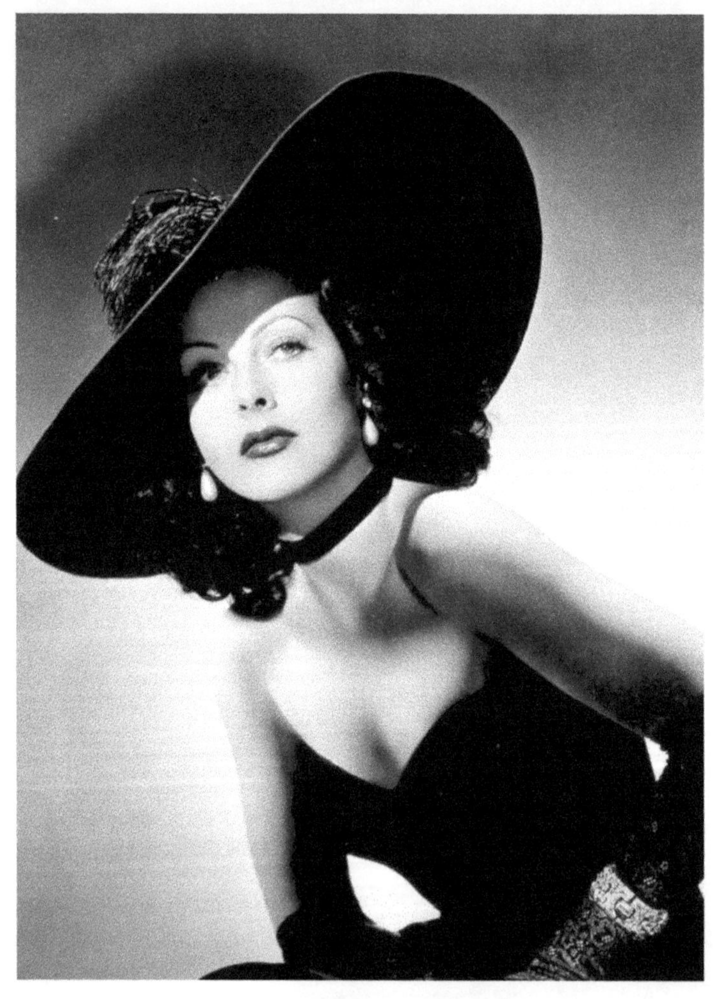

His niece was Hedy Lamarr,
Hollywood bombshell and inventor.

He was called, "a difficult, at times insufferable, character, a tireless self-promoter with the arrogance that often afflicts very short men." (He was 4'10". Or maybe 4'3". He said: "Genius and talent is hardly ever given to tall people.")

He "proposed nothing less than a total reformulation of art that would liberate it from the confines of the isolated aesthetic object." Being with him "was like touching an electric wire that bore the current of contemporary history."

Some sources say he was born in Romania in 1890. Wikipedia says he was born in Ukraine. I've read that he was Austrian. He was married in Poland. He moved to New York in 1926.

He is best known for designing Peggy Guggenheim's Art of this Century Gallery in 1942. His design featured paintings mounted on baseball bats, revolving paintings, and darkness.

He felt cheated by fate and maligned by some of his European fellow architects:

"They sailed in on the fame of overblown ado about the Bauhaus. And now they use their exalted chairs at Harvard and Yale to dominate architecture in America. They build and they scheme and they build and they scheme. They copy each other in arrogance. All my projects went down the drain in the depression. Had I waited like Mies or Gropius or Breuer, I would not have had to design the display windows for Saks Fifth Avenue to pay the rent or eat."

Ernest Hemingway would not shake his hand. "Hemingway froze in his bastard position and said, 'I do not shake hands with Germans or Austrians.' With that he turned around and away and disappeared into the café. The first World War was apparently not over for him yet. [It was 1925.] We have become Americans. He could have shaken hands with us now. But he is gone."

He wasn't very practical: "If Kiesler wants to hold two pieces of wood together, he pretends he's never heard of nails or screws. He tests the tensile strengths of various metal alloys, experiments with different methods and shapes, and after six months comes up with a very expensive device that holds two pieces of wood together almost as well as a screw." (Architectural Forum, 1947)

# SOME OF HIS PROPOSALS

- The Endless House (1924)*
- City in Space (1925)*
- Horizontal Skyscraper (1925)*
- Endless Theatre Without a Stage and Four-Dimensional Theatre (1926)*
- The Telemuseum (with walls designed as receiving screens for transmitted pictures – in 1927)*
- The Flying Desk (1930)*
- Nucleus House (1931)*
- Murals Without Walls (1936)*
- Vision Machine ("quasi-scientific, grandiose yet vague, ideogrammatic and poetic rather than diagrammatic") (1937)*
- Hall of Superstitions (1947)
- Tooth house (1948) *
- Grotto for Meditation (in the shape of a dolphin, underground) (1962)*

  * Unbuilt

Now we have buildings that look like fish, clouds, transformers. Rooms that look like Hebrew letters. Buildings incorporating what Kiesler called "biotechniques." But not then.

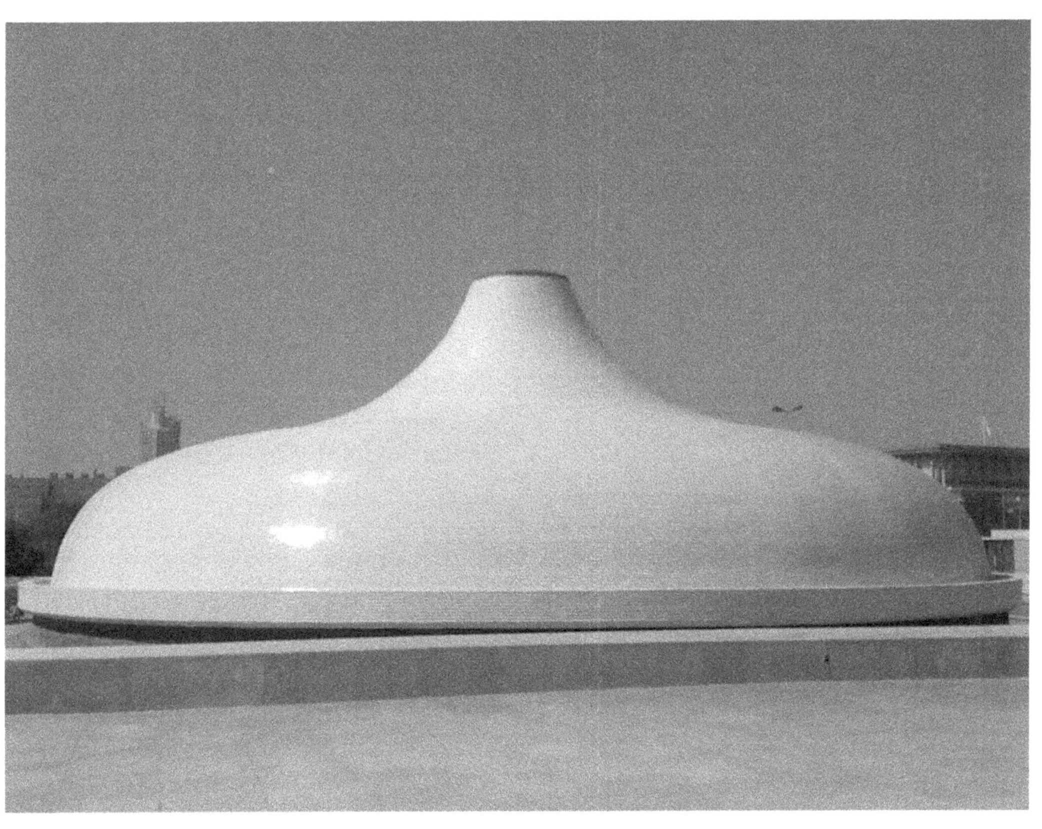

Just one of his buildings was ever built: The Shrine of the Book, opened in April 1965. In Jerusalem, it houses the Dead Sea Scrolls. "It's neither a woman's breast, nor an onion, nor a jar," he wrote.

# KIESLER HAD BIG IDEAS

"Form does not follow function; function follows vision. Vision follows reality."

"The place of art in society should be as necessary as the sun is to chlorophyll."

"The so-called artist must learn only one thing in order to be creative – not to resist himself, but to resist without exception every human, technical, social and economic factor that prevents him from being himself."

"Separatism, segregation, isolation in our social life must make way as never before to integration of purposes in all fields of endeavor. It will bring greater appreciation of our individuality, not conformity, simply because caring for each other is safeguarding the respect and esteem for every one of us."

"Poetry and art, the forerunners of social revolution, should now take the lead in promoting the content of this age of falling boundaries."

"Art can no longer live in mid-air nor architecture on the ground of business. That's over."

"Our Western world has been overrun by masses of art objects. What we really need is not more and more objects, but an objective."

"The materials are not the important matter, the important matter is how does one live, what new and inspirited life do they promote among the straight and curved lines?"

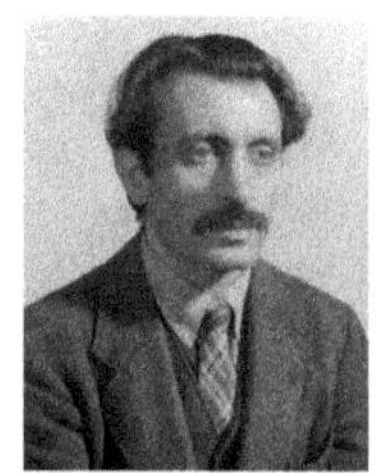

Gorky

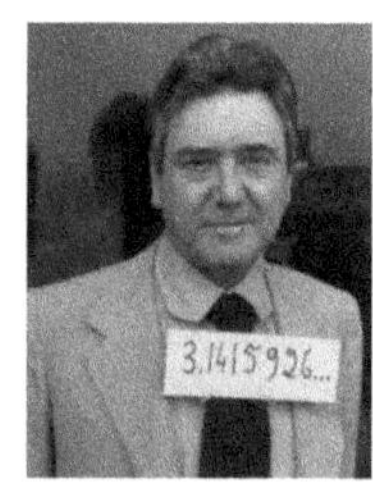



Matta

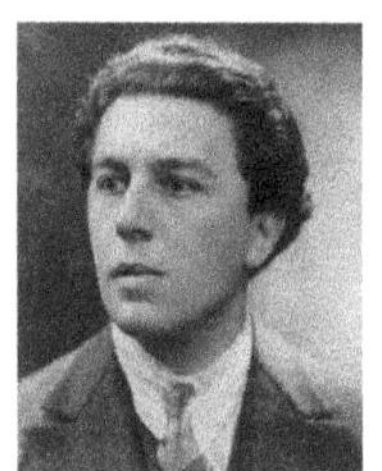

Breton

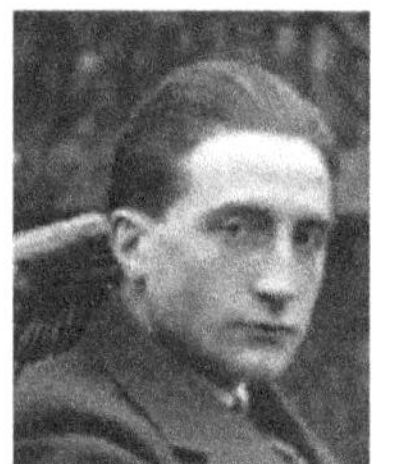

Duchamp

# THE MATTA AFFAIR

Kiesler was a close friend of Arshile Gorky, the painter. He accused Chilean artist Roberto Matta of triggering Gorky's suicide by having an affair with Gorky's wife. But Gorky had plenty of reasons to kill himself. His later years were filled with immense pain and heartbreak. His studio barn burned down, he had cancer, his neck was broken and his painting arm paralyzed in a car accident, and his marriage was already on the rocks.

According to the Kiesler Foundation:

> "After Gorky's suicide, painter Roberto Matta was excluded from Surrealism and returned to Europe. Kiesler was considered responsible for the purge of the Chilean artist because of a letter to Breton which remained undisclosed for many years. What did Kiesler do or say to harm Matta? Was he responsible or was he only a puppet in the hands of the mighty priests of Surrealism?"

One year after sending the Telegram, Duchamp was so mad at Kiesler for accusing Matta that they never spoke again.

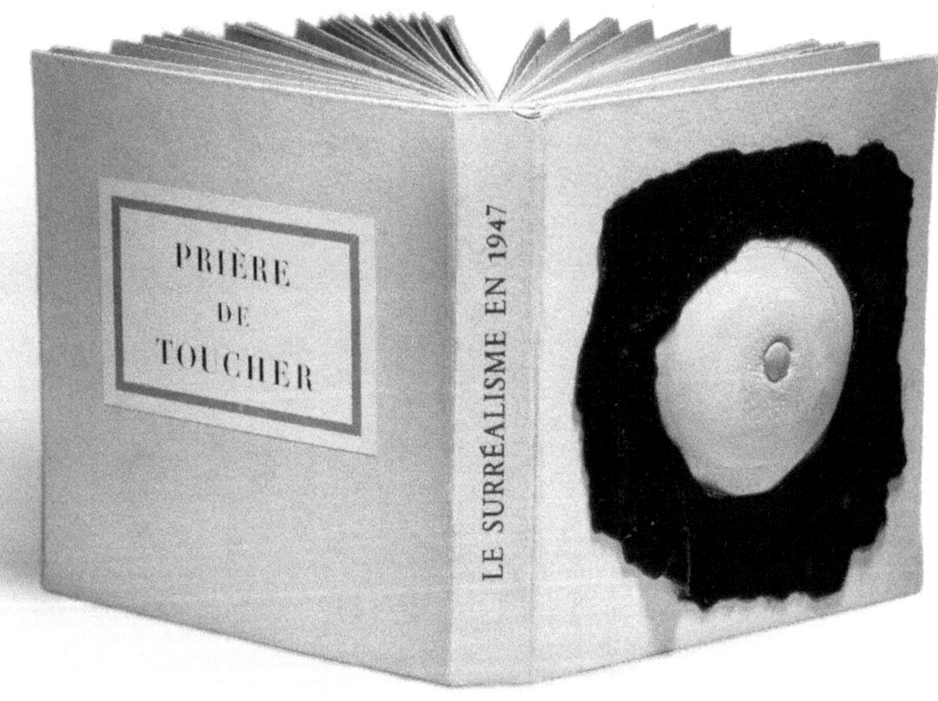

PRIÈRE
DE
TOUCHER
LE SURRÉALISME EN 1947

# CATALOGUE

"Dites Maeght m'envoyer catalogue."

That's the catalogue to "*Exposition Internationale du Surrealism Présentée par André Breton et Marcel Duchamp*".

Duchamp prepared a limited edition featuring a three-dimensional cover, pink with a pink foam rubber breast over an irregular piece of black velvet.  On the back cover a label: "Prière de toucher" : Please touch.

The Catalogue and show feature:

| | |
|---|---|
| Jean Arp | Jacqueline Lamba |
| Hans Bellmer | Roberto Matta |
| Victor Brauner | Joan Miro |
| André Breton | Isamu Noguchi |
| Alexander Calder | Roland Penrose |
| Leonora Carrington | Francis Picabia |
| Max Ernst | Remedios Varos |
| Alberto Giacometti | Hans Richter |
| Arshile Gorky | Kaye Sage |
| David Hare | Yves Tanguy |
| Wilfredo Lam | Dorothea Tanning |

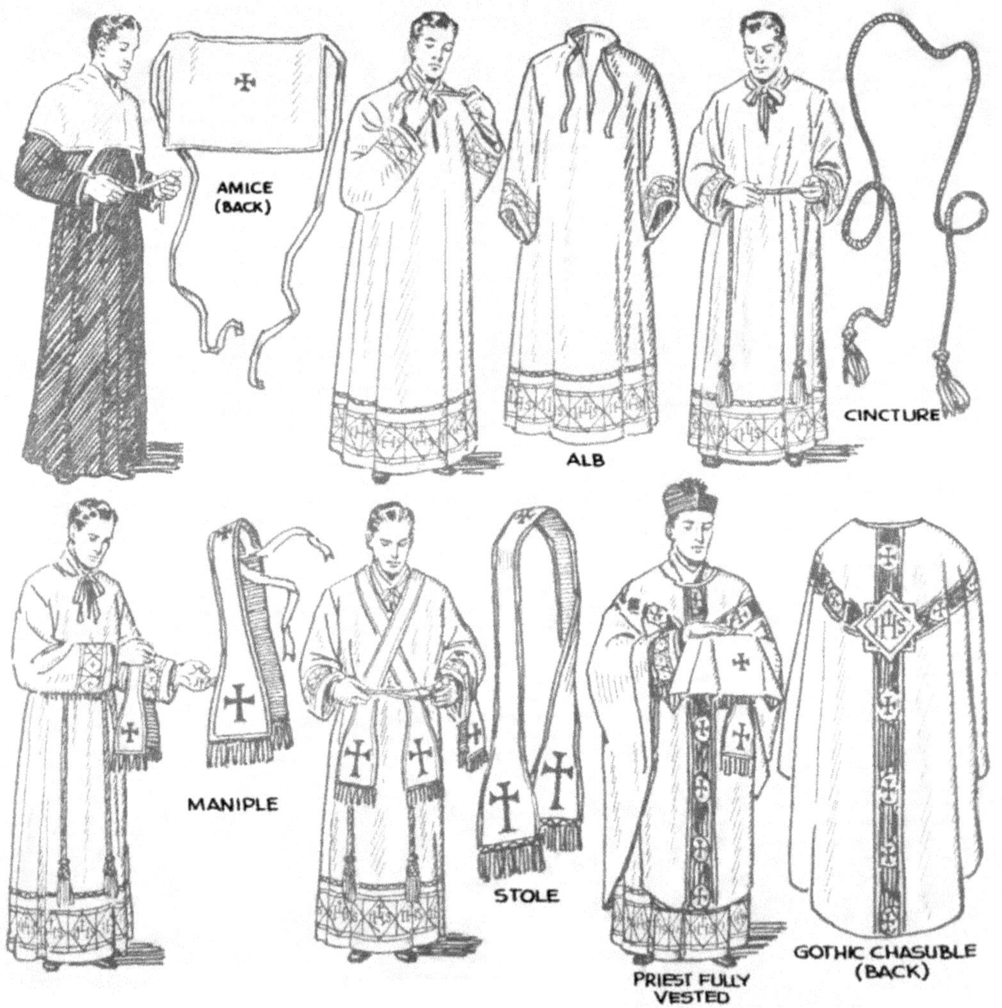

AMICE
(BACK)
ALB
CINCTURE
MANIPLE
STOLE
PRIEST FULLY
VESTED
GOTHIC CHASUBLE
(BACK)

# SUPERSTITIONS

For the show, Kiesler designed a Hall of Superstitions. The superstitions, sent by Benjamin Péret from Mexico, were listed in the catalogue:

- Leaving cupboards open brings good luck.

- The sight of an army officer brings bad luck. Hold your nose while he passes by.

- Make a wish when you see a priest beaten.

- To avoid ill luck, look away when you pass by a laundry.

- If you see a flag, turn away and spit to conjure the bad omen.

- When you go past a police station, sneeze loud to avoid misfortune.

- Throwing a crucifix in the first fire you light in the Autumn brings good luck.

"I prefer living and breathing to working. I do not consider that the work I have done could have any social importance in the future. So, if you like, my art would be that of living; each second, each breath is a work that is not recorded anywhere, that is neither visual nor cerebral.

It is a kind of constant euphoria."

–*Marcel Duchamp*

## GRATITUDE

Simone Perez

C. Nicolas

Robert Prowler

Daniel Ben-Horin

Diane Burk

Robert Langenbrunner

Wikimedia Commons

Marc Delany

Kate Stacey

Oliver Nash

First portrait of Marcel Duchamp copyright by the Estate of David Gahr

Published by Readymade Press • Paris, France

david@prowler.org